2-20-20

Dearest Katie,
    Blessings on your
Journey! See you in
4th, I'll be there
            Anna

A Miracle Worker's Primer

Anna Sweetnam Ph.D.

Champion the will of the ones you love

BALBOA
PRESS
A DIVISION OF HAY HOUSE

Balboa Press books may be ordered through booksellers or by contacting:

Balboa Press
A Division of Hay House
1663 Liberty Drive
Bloomington, IN 47403
www.balboapress.com
1-(877) 407-4847

Because of the dynamic nature of the Internet, any web addresses or links contained in this book may have changed since publication and may no longer be valid. The views expressed in this work are solely those of the author and do not necessarily reflect the views of the publisher, and the publisher hereby disclaims any responsibility for them.

The author of this book does not dispense medical advice or prescribe the use of any technique as a form of treatment for physical, emotional, or medical problems without the advice of a physician, either directly or indirectly. The intent of the author is only to offer information of a general nature to help you in your quest for emotional and spiritual well-being. In the event you use any of the information in this book for yourself, which is your constitutional right, the author and the publisher assume no responsibility for your actions.

Any people depicted in stock imagery provided by Thinkstock are models, and such images are being used for illustrative purposes only.
Certain stock imagery © Thinkstock.

ISBN: 978-1-4525-5835-6 (hc)
ISBN: 978-1-4525-5833-2 (sc)
ISBN: 978-1-4525-5834-9 (e)

Library of Congress Control Number: 2012916768

Printed in the United States of America

Balboa Press rev. date: 12/7/2012

Contents

Preface

Many of us can admit it, our lives are not perfect.

Our family life is certainly not perfect and particular challenges make life absolutely unfair. Looking at the bigger picture, we can also admit we are here to fully experience life along with all these unfair life challenges. Life lesson after life lesson remain unresolved, acted out, and constantly recreating frustrations and difficulties on all levels. Does life really have to be so difficult?

May this book be used as a welcome invitation into the Keller Family home, as you witness and experience life challenges and opportunities. Use it as a primer (you know, that old-fashioned term for an elementary school book?) to see yourself, to see family members, to see your children, and to see your friends all coping with the exhilarating journey of their life experiences.

The material presented in this primer can appear to be somewhat provocative especially for the third dimensional reader (read on to find out what this label truly means). The information and tools described are meant to be provocative in order to shift you from one way of thinking into a new and hopefully better way. Sometimes we just aren't ready for the new thought, new information, or new idea when we think we are, but the process may become revealing and enlightening.

Use this primer as an educational tool. Learn from the Keller family experience as they discover the sorely needed inner discipline and use this as a navigational tool through life's uncharted territory. Take their lead and champion the will of the ones you love. Be a Miracle Worker today!

Introduction

The Miracle Worker, what an incredible story! A true to life story about a little girl named Helen Keller who became deaf and blind at the tender young age of 18 months due to a childhood illness. Helen's parents anxiously search for a special education teacher to work with the now six-year-old girl and her very dysfunctional lifestyle, which has always been accepted and tolerated as normal living in the Keller household. The miracle worker is Miss Annie Sullivan, Helen's teacher, who had the daunting task of reaching the essence, the 'Spirit' of little lost Helen.

Miss Annie Sullivan was an orphan and attended Boston's Perkins School for the Blind. She lost her own sight as a young child, although her story ended a little different from that of Helen. With the help of several operations her vision was restored. Education was very important to Miss Sullivan and she graduated as valedictorian of her class in 1886. A year later, she acquired her first teaching position. She was hired to tutor Helen Keller, a blind and deaf six year old. Miss Sullivan became known as _The Miracle Worker_ and was Helen's permanent companion, teacher and guide.

As you read on you will begin to notice a constant common thread of the Divine's handiwork. This thread, a very intricate weave, will be revealed throughout the story. Miss Annie is the hero of the story. Miss Annie's life was beautifully and purposefully orchestrated, a truly Divine orchestration, to become the miracle worker for the Keller household. As the newcomer to the Keller family, Miss Annie takes on the challenges, the contest of wills, of not just her student, Helen, but of the entire Keller family. It is, after all, what a true 'miracle worker' would undertake. In the end, it's not just Helen who ends up 'seeing the light'.

Most of the text of _A Miracle Worker's Primer_ comes from the movie, _The Miracle Worker_. I took advantage of the Hollywood movie version and the storyline embellishments, written by the screen writer/author of the original play, William Gibson, and all the dramas found within. Truth be told, it is William Gibson who is the original Miracle Worker. Without his brilliance and foresight, the Helen Keller story would not have been portrayed with such depth and knowledge of human nature. There are many Miracle Workers in the world; the best are probably our children's teachers, like Miss Annie, Helen's teacher. Miracles happen daily at the hands of individuals willing to contest the will of a neighbor, friend, student and most importantly and difficult - a loved one.

It was William Gibson who captured the essence of the Keller family as a primer for all of us who are willing to take his lead and learn how to champion the will of a loved one. As a writer, the Angels were truly with him, and he knew it.

"Writers go bad when the angels desert them. Dylan Thomas was a marvelous poet who drank himself to death. Somewhere along the way, the angel left him. An angel has left me too, but the writing angel is still with me, and that's the thing where I feel the most alive—at least while I'm doing it. I started out to be a writer and I'm still a writer—not bad."
William Gibson, Hartford Courant 2005

For best results while working with this primer, be sure to follow along with the original black and white film version of _The Miracle Worker_, starring Anne Bancroft and Patty Duke. This film reveals many life lessons we can explore together, encouraging the discovery of life possibilities, life tools and lifetime solutions. Indeed, many of the Keller family dramas we have all personally experienced. By taking the Keller family's lead, we can also benefit by digging out some of those rusty, dusty tools at the bottom of our very own 'toolbox'.

Each and every one of us has had life experiences geared and dedicated specifically toward forming the essence of who we are. Each day, each minute of each year, we act and react from a culmination of earlier life experiences that combine to make up our character. Never in those minutes should we ever underestimate the perfection of our life experiences. Nor should we ever underestimate the perfection we are. Every coincidence, every piece of good luck, every piece of bad luck, every impossibility and every improbability contains a Divine link to the person you are and to the person you will become. Nothing has been left to chance. Like a snowflake; no two lives are exactly the same. Are we not supposed to do something special with these very well planned out experiences? Can we discover our true life purpose by taking the time to open the map of our lives and notice the roads we have taken, the detours, side streets and the freeways of where we have been, and where we could go?

I too, have encountered life opportunities and lessons to pull from my own well of wisdom in order to write this primer. From my personal life experiences, to my vast and unique educational background, the Universe certainly has had a Divine hand in directing me toward *The Miracle Worker* story. It wasn't until I completed writing this primer that I truly understood the depth of how this "miracle" story has influenced my life.

With a Masters Degree in Education teaching the Emotionally and Socially challenged community, it didn't take me long to realize that classroom management wasn't reaching the core, the essence of the child. The children were, in a sense, virtually deaf and blind themselves and not one little bit of education could come about until the child's Spirit was reached. And how do you do that exactly, reach Spirit? When the child is in their Spirit, they are free from life distractions and human drama. With this new found recognition they can now build upon their life lessons as a blueprint for fulfilling their potential, purpose and passions. With this different point of focus, they begin to gather up the facts of their lives, empowered to create the life they were meant to lead: the grander, bigger plan. Anything less is chaos, dysfunction and confusion.

The big question remained - 'How do you do that?' How do you reach that internal place, the essence of an individual? For me, the answer was in discovering *everything* about how to reach the human Spirit. Hmm...Where do you get information on the human Spirit?

Metaphysics, of course! You can't truly reach a child or any adult/child by telling them what to do, when to do it and why. You reach an individual's Spirit by slowing down, being present and drawing out from them 'what? when? why? and who?' Asking pointed questions forces the individual to connect and reach deep within themselves for answers, solutions and good ideas. You must continue to ask questions until you can reach an honest and workable consensus. Together you can negotiate a win/win solution, and remind the child, for example, 'curfew is at midnight'. Each party feels mutually respected, and an amicable decision can be made.

I knew this whole philosophy and outlook would change the course of my life forever. My family and friends, it seems, would no longer be my family and friends. They would be functioning in what I will call a 3DL state, or the Third Dimension Lifestyle - a mind-set where you don't have to think or consider the true depth of your heart and mind's needs or wants. This mind-set is an easy place to coast in life, learning to settle for less and never challenging the will, *their will* - their Spirit. I, and others like me, would grow and evolve into a 4DL state, the Fourth Dimension Lifestyle. 3DLers would not want to know the differences; they would only ridicule anyone in 4DL. They would not understand the Fourth Dimension and I would forever be the reminder of the integrity they know they could possess. For those of us who do understand, this is how we live our lives. For those of you who want to know more about how to live a 4DL, Spiritual state - I welcome you into the home of Helen Keller as a witness to Miss Annie Sullivan's miracle worker teachings.

To simplify, throughout the book you will notice a constant thread of discussion revealing what I refer to as the Four Dimension of living. Specifically in *A Miracle Worker's Primer*, the Third and Fourth Dimensions will be concentrated upon and discussed. Brief definitions of the four dimensions are:

1st dimensional lifestyle refers to the mineral kingdom
2nd dimensional lifestyle refers to the animal and plant kingdom
3rd dimensional lifestyle or 3DL, refers to the human kingdom
4th dimensional lifestyle or 4DL, refers to the Spiritual kingdom

As the Universe would have it, on my own consciousness path of purpose, I created a Holistic Wellness Center called <u>The Conscious Connection</u>. The real beauty of the Center is revealed in the individuals who visit. They want to *know*, or else they wouldn't have walked in the door. They are looking, searching and sometimes they aren't really sure what they are looking and searching for, but they did walk in of their own accord. They may have evolved enough to have one foot straddling the 3DL and the other foot in the 4DL. They are ready for a life awakening, a Spiritual experience.

Who will be the one who would challenge their belief system? Someone who would have the courage to stand up to what feels like a threat to their very existence, to the beliefs and perceptions they currently hold? Take the Keller family, could they actually be ready for the challenge and not realize that what they really want is someone to contest their will? They understand that something profound is missing, but don't yet realize what they are missing is their own Spirit; they are missing the 4DL. Like Miss Annie Sullivan:

> *"It now remains my pleasant task to direct and mould the beautiful intelligence that is beginning to stir in the child-soul."*
> **Annie Sullivan. Story of My Life. p 260.**

For me, my days are filled with the joy and passion working with the individuals who are searching for 4DL *"...to direct and mould the beautiful intelligence that is beginning to stir..."* They are tired of being tired, living the 3DL. Much more difficult is the task of reaching individuals like Helen Keller, who don't necessarily want transformation. Helen didn't walk into Miss Sullivan's office and say, 'Transform me!' It was Helen's parents, her guardians, who asked for assistance. In a case such as this, transformation may be a little more difficult initially, as we witness the challenges Miss Annie underwent while merely contesting Helen's will, but which proved nonetheless rewarding.

There is so much for all of us to know and do-- really. Each and every one of us has important work to do. We all have neighbors and friends that we know live horrid 3DL and we sit back and do nothing. Especially frightening, is being aware of children who are suffering at the hands of the adults in their lives. These 3DL adult/children hurt those younger than themselves. This particular 3DL person could be any adult/child: a teacher, a neighbor, a relative or maybe even you yourself. Understand the ripple effect this damaging life approach has upon the community, and upon the World at large. Why we choose to accept and tolerate this behavior is not through living the 4DL way. If you are aware of someone who needs assistance and you choose to do nothing to help, understand you are living 3DL. Human fears override your Spiritual quests.

Nothing in life will go right until life *is* right. There is a lot to do, much cleaning up at hand, and many magnificent miracles to reveal.

> *"It was no doubt because of my ignorance that I rushed in where more experienced Angels fear to tread."*
> **Annie Sullivan, The Story of My Life. p 283.**

What miracle will you create today? Risk taking a bold stand for a child or adult/child in your life; they depend on it, they are crying out for it. We all cry for it. Dare to be a miracle worker.

What a Miracle Worker Would Share

There is no doubt the Keller family lived a very difficult and dysfunctional lifestyle. There is no doubt that *many* families today experience very difficult and dysfunctional lifestyles. Who are the miracle workers for families today? Sorely lacking, there seems to be little evidence of parents championing the will of their children. What lack do today's adult/authority figures reveal, when they are unable to encourage, empower, and teach children to be self-sufficient and autonomous? Could it be that adult/authority figures lack their *own* will, their *own* Spirit to draw from?

The answer is yes. Overall, adult/authority figures, be it in a family, corporate family or business family, may fear they will not be loved if they assert their will and challenge the will of others. Feelings of rejection, abandonment, not being loved, not being lovable… consume and paralyze the individuals with no positive result at hand. Feelings of indifference, irresolution, indecision, vacillation and wishy-washiness are experienced.

We may not like this truth and even feel threatened as these beliefs are challenged throughout this handbook. There needs to be will power, force of will, moral courage, self-discipline, strength of purpose, conviction, determination and desire.

Be the adult/authority figure in your own life. Leave behind the emotions of guilt, shame, anxiety, doubt, and confusion... don't let these emotions be your daily examples. Rather, hang onto your hopes, dreams and aspirations; stay true to yourself. Never deter from the role of a miracle worker.

Hope whispers and encourages... try one more time.

3DL or 4DL is a choice; which lifestyle do you choose?

Will— *Synonym*—will power, force of will, moral courage, self discipline, strength of purpose, conviction, determination, desire.

OR

Will— *Antonym*—indifference, irresolution, indecision, vacillation, wishy-washiness

Players

Miss Annie Sullivan – Helen's Teacher

Helen Keller - Blind and Deaf Child

Captain Keller – Helen's Dad

Kate Keller – Helen's Mom

Jimmy Keller – Helen's Half Brother

Aunt Ev – Helen's Aunt

Scene One

A Journey

The family Doctor is in the Keller home inspecting baby Helen's health.

Kate: Will my girl be all right?
Family Doctor: By morning she'll be knockin' down Captain Keller's fences again.

Welcome into the Keller family home. In the opening scene of <u>The Miracle Worker</u>, we see two concerned parents acting very 'human' about baby Helen's health and wellbeing. Just given a clean bill of health from the family Doctor, the Keller family is unaware that they have just embarked on a new 'life lesson' with their daughter. 'Life Lesson' is a phrase used when we take the time to consciously connect with what our life purpose on this planet could actually be about. Life lessons are usually questioned when wrestling with the age-old mysteries of life - the awareness of self. We realize that life is bigger than we could ever have imagined, and we then begin to ask questions such as: What is this thing called life about? Who am I? Is there a purpose? Is there a bigger picture? What is *my* purpose?

For the Keller family, the life lesson will be based around a non-seeing, non-hearing child and everything that kind of handicapped lifestyle could involve. Or, should the statement really read: For the Keller family, the life lesson will be based around a non-seeing, non-hearing child and everything that kind of handicapped lifestyle could *evolve*?

You may have noticed and recognized as a child in elementary school, or maybe as a high school student, the personal trials and tragedies many families, friends and neighbors endure. Your grandparents may have personal struggles to overcome; maybe your own parents, a sibling, or maybe you yourself are struggling with a personal life lesson. What about stories you have heard through the years about a student or peer? Life lessons usually focus around major life changing issues such as personal, emotional and especially Spiritual dramas. Maybe there are certain relationships with family or friends, or a career challenge, money issues or personal health concerns. As a witness to 'others' experiencing life challenges, it's easy to realize no one goes unscathed; everyone is experiencing some sort of personal human/Spiritual growth.

The purpose and function of this book is to use the Keller family story as a personal primer. This primer will serve as an excellent tool for anyone's personal toolbox, and for anyone who wants to make a difference - to be a miracle worker. Use the example of the Keller story as a study in life; we know all the family members, we already know the family challenges. We have the benefit of knowing the story from the beginning to the end. Unlike our personal life story, we don't know what will happen - not even ten minutes from now. With the Keller family we have the advantage of both foresight and hindsight information. Let's just pretend the Kellers are our neighbors and we can watch from a distance, we can look from the outside in. Let's take this unique vantage point for our own educational benefit and well being.

As mentioned above, many of us already know the Keller story from the beginning to the end; let's sum up the life lesson aspect. We can look at life lessons in one of two ways. We can see life lessons as a challenge or as a blessing. Here we have a family with a deaf and blind child, an incredible life challenge - a life challenge, or a blessing? If the Keller family takes the life lesson as a challenge, they will experience life as overwhelming, tiring, and burdensome. Anyone would be able to tell by their energy, their overall drained enthusiasm and the attitude that they carry the weight of the challenge heavily upon themselves. How they talk, how they hold themselves - their body posture, their mannerisms; these are all indicators of how life is a challenge. Worse yet is how they are a burden to their community and the community's resources.

If, on the other hand, the Kellers see their situation as one of being 'blessed' with this experience, they have the opportunity to create a ripple effect within their neighborhood and town, becoming role models for the blind and the deaf community. This particular type of family, displaying this type of attitude, would naturally take on the responsibilities and be accountable for their personal situation. They would not become a burden to their community or the communities' resources. All this in a wee little town in Tuscumbia, Alabama; a place few have ever heard of, a place few have traveled to. A simple nobody family! How incredible they were, with Miss Annie Sullivan, the miracle worker's help!

How about you? How about the life lesson your family is experiencing? Fill in the paragraph to see about your family:

> The **ABC** family (your family name), is blessed with this life challenge and can become the ripple effect within the community as a role model for **123** (your life lesson). All this in a wee little town in **LMNOP** (name of your town); a place few have ever heard of, a place few have traveled to. A simple nobody family! How incredible they are, with **XYZ**, the miracle worker's help!

Reflecting for a moment, has this thought of looking at your life from this very different perspective touched your inner being, stirred your heart? How do you feel? Did you feel the shift of seeing the one perspective and then again seeing this new and different perspective as a warm heartfelt feeling? Having the vantage point of the Keller story gives us a clearer opportunity to consciously connect with the bigger picture of life, the grander plan. As if we could hold all of Helen's life in the palm of our hand, we can see past the daily grind to a bigger picture, the Universe's hand. A life plan that is bigger than any one of us. We can come to realize that the better part of the plan is being orchestrated by something bigger than and greater than - us.

Possible Miracle Worker Dialog—Context Sensitive

You most likely know of someone who is experiencing a challenging time in their life. As a third party watching and observing from the outside you may be able to notice more than those in the throes of the experience. Although context sensitive, would you ever be able to suggest... *'Have you noticed the Universe's Hand in your current experience? A life plan that is bigger than any one of us. We can come to realize that the better part of the plan is being orchestrated by something bigger than and greater than -- us. Our job is to jockey around the grand plan. Like a chess game... what pawn will you move so you won't be checkmated?'*

Incredibly, as part of the plan, we have all been given the gift of choice, we can make wiser choices and decisions as we play this game of life, or we can make not-so-wise choices and decisions. We can celebrate life, or we can celebrate with pity-parties. This is also a choice.

Having a better understanding of this game of life, we might be able to embrace and welcome the idea of personal life lessons. Knowing this doesn't make life any easier, but it could encourage you to take on life challenges gallantly, with as much grace as possible. You could be your own miracle worker, the hero in your own life lesson, in your own family, in your own community.

Something bigger than you is happening on this planet, something more than just a simple human being lifestyle, better known as a third dimensional lifestyle, or 3DL for short. The ultimate learning curve for all of us is to reveal and consider the benefits of a Spiritual-vibrating lifestyle, known as a fourth dimensional lifestyle, or 4DL for short. For now, simply hold onto the 'heartfelt feeling' shift you just experienced as we move through the incredible - *The Miracle Worker* story.

In the opening paragraph you probably noticed the original statement about the 'two concerned parents acting very 'human'. Throughout the book there will be references about individuals who are acting and reacting in a very expected, human manner. These individuals exist at a simple human vibration level, and as mentioned in the prior paragraph, this will be referred to as the third dimensional lifestyle or 3DL. This lifestyle would be basically represented in everyday normal human behavior. 3DL behaviors are what most humans generally exhibit.

Typical human reactions and overreactions of the third dimension lifestyle, 3DL, includes heavy emotional responses such as fearfulness, anxiety, stressful living, jealousies, over-extending the self, enabling, co-dependencies, low self-esteem... These states of mind are a few of the emotional dramas also uncovered within *The Miracle Worker*.

Concurrently we will also be drawing out the Spiritual aspects of what will be referred to as the Spiritual vibration, or the fourth dimensional lifestyle, 4DL. In this dimension we will reveal and illustrate humans with stronger personalities - those who possess personal power, exhibit higher self-esteem, trustworthiness, unconditional love, forgiveness, reveal calmer dispositions, who are joyful and grateful, and who act more like heroes, or miracle workers...

There has been some attention directed toward Miss Annie and Helen through the years, including two additional movie remakes of the Helen Keller story. No matter how often you view the movie, it's easy to be awed by the heartwarming feeling experienced when we watch *The Miracle Worker*. That fourth dimensional 'feeling', 4DL, as if the Angels were all around supporting with an electrical bolt of energy - a Divine touch. We've all felt it before, a lighting-up feeling, like a chill up the neck or goose bumps and a far off chant of *"Ahhhh..."* This would be the sign, the confirmation if you will, to celebrate and sing with the Angels when you experience the fourth dimensional, 4DL heartfelt feeling - *"Ahhhh!..."*

Not much has been written about the depth and scope of what this chronicled story can provide in terms of moving us from personal human growth and development, to personal Spiritual growth and development, from 3DL to 4DL. Amazing to think the Helen Keller story has been in front of us for half a century and has not lost its ability to move us. Of course, it is much easier to put off and avoid the truths we see about ourselves in everyday life, let alone to recognize them as they are acted out in *The Miracle Worker* story. We have convinced ourselves that life is easier when we simply avoid, allowing ourselves to pretend everything is fine; a common example of 3DL. Using the story of *The Miracle Worker* as an incredible tool, we will discover that 4DL living is fun to explore; a simpler way of life and, bottom-line, the preferred way to live. Remember - whenever 4DL is revealed to you - hold on to and welcome the 'heartfelt feeling', the 4DL feeling. Listen for the Angels. You have heard them before. All together now, *"Ahhhh..."*

What a Miracle Worker Would Share

Miss Annie, in the story *The Miracle Worker*, has already done all the hard work for us. She's made it easy for us. Not only did she live this incredible life, but it has all been chronicled and miraculously expressed in a movie format for the purpose of our personally dissecting it. All we have to do is welcome the gift and give ourselves the permission to explore personal human/Spirit drama, 3DL/4DL, and admit how similar our own family life story is to the Keller family - and we aren't even deaf or blind. Or are we?

Consider observing and welcoming the concept of the 'bigger' picture of life; we are here experiencing life lessons. Welcome this process, the choice is ours: to live a human drama-filled existence, a 3DL, or a Spiritual drama-free existence, a 4DL. Always remembering this is a choice.

Could you feel the 4DL shift again, just now? I could hear the Angels for a second. It sounded like *"Ah-h"* and then there was a shift back and I didn't hear them anymore. Accordingly, this means the information was *almost* absorbed by you, the reader. You were half way there - not quite buying into the 4DL. When you really experience the 4DL feeling you'll feel it like a chill up your neck or goose bumps, you'll come to know it as singing with the Angels. This 4DL is a welcome feeling of a true moment of celebration. Feel it, *"Ahhhh!"*

You may not know it yet, but what we 3DLers really want most in life is the celebration. We actually want a lifetime of these celebrations. These moments that are lit up so strong and so powerful, they can frighten us. More often than not, these moments are so powerful, so overwhelming, we may not have even consciously connected to the moment or moments. Most often we shrug off the emotion and dismiss the feeling, the chill, and the goose bumps. We unfortunately deny the powerful people that we are. Like trying to hold onto a hand full of water in the palm of our hand, the water illusively escapes. Imagine walking around all day with a chill up your neck or all day goose bumps and shivers. Chilling even to think about, and ironically, the feeling we really strive for as human beings. 4DL is preferred, celebration is preferred. It may be scary to think we could actually hold this feeling in the palm of our hand every day, all day, passionately blissful. Don't fight it, go with it, feel it thoroughly - welcome the chill. Angels, *"Ahhhh!"*

Let's look at the next scene and discover life lesson potential, even if we aren't quite ready to see how the Keller story relates to us. Remember now, we're pretending the Keller family are our neighbors and we can watch from a distance, we can look from the outside in. We're going to take this vantage point, as if peering over their fence, for our own educational benefit and well being. We may even tiptoe into their living room.

3DL or 4DL is a choice, which lifestyle do you choose?

Welcome– *Synonyms*–gladly received, wanted, accepted, at home, comfortable, agreeable, delightful, pleasing, gratifying, inviting, engaging, winning, enticing, charming

OR

Welcome– *Antonyms*–snub, rebuff, cold shoulder, brush off, unwanted, excluded.

Scene Two

Embrace Life, Embrace Life Lessons

The family Doctor has just left and Captain Keller is walking him to the door. Kate makes a startling discovery and panics screaming for the Captain.

Kate: Helen? Helen! Cap'n! (screaming) Cap'n! Will you come?
Captain Keller: Katie! What is it? What's wrong?
Kate: Look! She can't see. Look at her eyes. She can't see. Or hear. When I screamed she didn't blink. Not an eyelash!
Captain Keller: Helen. Helen!
Kate: She can't hear you!
Captain Keller: Helen!

Make a quick spin of your personal rolodex, who do you know who has personal health issues as a current life challenge? Who in your family is afflicted with a disability? Maybe a child you know has ADD/ADHD, Dyslexia, or is Autistic? Worse, maybe you know of someone who is struggling with childhood Cancer or Diabetes? Who of your family members has the biggest health issues, with tantrums in tow? Is it a sister or brother? Maybe a younger or older sibling has health issues? They could be 4, 14, 44 or 74? Or possibly a parent who still hasn't decided to grow up and is constantly haunted with 3DL human drama, as if they have a black cloud hanging over their head. Nothing goes right. Maybe there is an adult/child with an addiction and like Helen's parents; your family feels both helpless and hopeless. No one knows exactly what to do. You are, in essence, in the depth of 3DL. In view of the overall scope of life changing challenges/opportunities to choose from, the pickings are ripe for learning and pushing through some great life lessons.

How have you been blessed with life challenges? The third dimensional lifestyle belief system, 3DL, would have you believe this: what a terrible life you have with this challenge, along with that sad shake of the head exclaiming, *'How unfortunate…'* Indeed, what a struggle, what a problem, and what a headache you are experiencing this lifetime. Taking offense to all of this, you exclaim: *'Why me?'* You may even be thinking: *'Where is the blessing in this? This is not a blessing!'*

These thoughts and statements are all very personal human 3DL thoughts and very real statements. These types of beliefs will keep you in a place of despair and confusion, thereby creating a lifestyle of self pity, dependency and neediness for anyone who will listen. You will relate to others from the past days, years and months with your particular wounds. You may have even noticed how you connect with individuals who have similar wounds and a victim mentality. You commiserate, relate, reminisce, ruminate, and essentially exist in a past state, relating in unhealthy ways to your wounds rather than to a proactive, creative, clever existence and lifestyle.

Possible Miracle Worker Dialog-- Context Sensitive

A 4DL'er would share…*'Looks like you are having a Spiritual Experience. Life can be tough, rough and certainly not fair! So many seem to have life easier, they seem lucky. Although you might admit some are worse off with terrible life stories. Is it a roll of the dice? Maybe they were dealt a better hand of cards? Does it really matter? Not so much, but what matters and what is more important is how we handle it.'*

We could look at the broader picture and decide it doesn't matter what we experience or are about to experience. We might decide to enjoy the thrill of the life journey. We could enjoy the little things like eating, sleeping, playing, using our senses and especially being sensual - all the bodily functions. We could relish loving as well as hating and everything in between. Maybe this thing called life with all its challenges, joys and opportunities is worth all the ups and downs, the highs and lows. We would rather have the experiences or be a (((poof))) in the ethers and have no experiences at all. Consider…living is what we are here for! Success is how well we handle the role we have decided to take on.

The Fourth Dimensional Lifestyle belief system, 4DL, would turn those negative thoughts inside out. You would be able to embrace with and see the opportunities revealing themselves as blessings. Enamored with the challenge, you exclaim, *'We have been chosen, we are blessed.'* You would know you were selected, even chosen for this particular life experience. What an incredible 'strong soul' to take on such a challenge. You and your family are one of – *them.* Many have been selected, although few are chosen, even fewer take on the challenge. 4DL'ers take on the challenge/opportunity.

Do you hear the Angels? *"Ahhhh!..."* They are proud of you for taking on the challenges and opportunities.

In the case of the life lessons illustrated in *The Miracle Worker*, Helen is both deaf and blind. Her parents don't know what to do; they don't know how to help her. They feel both helpless and hopeless; they feel inadequate and not up to the task. They are in a sense, both deaf and blind themselves and in the depth of 3DL. Using *The Miracle Worker* story as a personal primer, symbolically consider all members in every family as deaf and blind. Each family that solely lives and experiences 3DL is a family whose members are both deaf and blind, symbolically speaking, of course.

What a Miracle Worker Would Share

Remember that 3DL includes human drama. Again, typical reactions and overreactions of the third dimension lifestyle, (3DL) include emotional responses such as general fears, anxieties, stressors, jealousy, co-dependencies, over extending the self, enabling, and low self-esteem. In many ways these labels keep you and your family deaf and blind to the issues. Not until you consciously connect and choose to observe, to look, will this veil come off. Until you actually want to look to take the next step, you are virtually acting as deaf and blind as Helen. Your family is in just as much chaos as the Keller family. Your family experiences just as much dysfunction as the Kellers. Not until you want to truly look, speak up and take action, and not until you consciously connect, will you overcome this 3DL family drama. What would we see if we tiptoed into your family's living room?

Miss Annie was the one who was able to reach Helen on a 4DL level; her parents did not and could not. Without minimizing the incredible challenge of having a child who cannot hear or see, Mr. and Mrs. Keller were unable to reach Helen's Spirit, the essence of Helen. Most parents today are unable to reach the essence, the Spirit of their own children, and their children most likely can see and hear normally. Worse off are the families that actually have a child who is afflicted with a handicap, some life-threatening malady. The intensity of these life lessons are extremely powerful and overwhelming challenges/opportunities for these families, as we continue to recognize the parallel examples of the Keller family to our own.

Looking at the bigger life picture, *The Miracle Worker* story reveals the moment when the Kellers have been introduced to the challenge of their life lesson. Maybe you have already been introduced to your own life lesson challenge/opportunity or challenges/opportunities. For you, you will be able to benefit and relate to the Keller family on a much more personal level. Embrace your life and your life lessons, which are the exact reasons why you are experiencing this life. Read between the lines of the Keller story and adopt their life experiences as handy new tools in your toolbox. Use their strength as an example and role model for you and your personal life challenges/opportunities. Embrace the idea that you are one of the chosen ones. All of us have been chosen; you have been given a gift, you have been selected to take on such a life challenge/opportunity. How incredibly brave you are with such courage, a 'strong soul.' Drum rolls please, Angels—*"Ahhhh!..."*

3DL or 4DL is a choice, which lifestyle do you choose?

Embrace–   *Synonyms*–include, involve, contain, embody, consolidate, comprise, incorporate, cover, encompass

OR

Embrace–   *Antonyms*–omit, delete, exclude, ignore, disregard

Scene Three

The Magic of Chaos

In this scene the Keller family is visiting together in the living room. Exasperated, the Kellers banter back and forth about just what to do for Helen!

Aunt Ev: Arthur? Arthur, something ought to be done for that child.
Captain Keller: A refreshin' suggestion. What?
Aunt Ev: Why, this very famous Perkins School in Boston they're just supposed to do wonders.
Captain Keller: The child's been to specialists everywhere. They couldn't help her in Baltimore or Washington, could they?
Kate: I think the Captain will write to the Perkins School soon.
Captain Keller: Katie, how many times can you let them break your heart?
Kate: Any number of times.
Aunt Ev: What, child?
Kate: As long as there's the least chance for her to see or hear.
Captain Keller: What, child? There isn't! Now I must finish here.
Kate: I think with your permission, Captain I would like to write to the Perkins School.
Captain Keller: I said no, Katie.
Aunt Ev: Why writing does no harm, Arthur only a little bitty letter. To see if they can help her.
Captain Keller: They can't.
Kate: We won't know that to be a fact Captain until after you write.
Captain Keller: Kate. (Helen knocks Captain Keller's papers to the floor.)
Captain: I might as well try to work in a hen yard as in this house. (Baby cries)
Brother Jimmy: You really ought to put her away, Father.
Kate: What?

Brother Jimmy: *Some asylum. It's the kindest thing.*
Aunt Ev: *Why she's your sister, James, not a nobody--*
Brother Jimmy: *Half-sister and half... mentally defective, she can't keep herself clean. It's not pleasant to see her about all the time.*
Kate: *Do you dare? Complain of what you can see?*
Captain Keller: *This discussion's at an end. The house is at sixes and sevens from morning to night over the child. I want some peace here, I don't care how, but one way we won't have it is by rushin' about the country every time someone hears of a new quack. I'm as sensible to this affliction as...*

This is just another day in the life of the Keller family. Is this how it is in your home? Is there chaos, bedlam and overall human drama with no quick solutions available, just constant arguments and disagreements as the current course of inter-action? Who's the loudest screamer and complainer in your home? Notice signs of 3DL? Who are the less boisterous, subdued individuals who observe life and react by keeping the best interest of all in mind? Notice signs of 4DL in these individuals.

Have you ever noticed, in any size family: be it a personal family, a classroom family or a corporate family, the disposition of different personalities is virtually identical in each of these families? Like a pecking order... there are those that are strong and loud, wielding misguided power over those who are weaker, vulnerable and misunderstood. Think of the neighbors to your right, and consider their pecking order. Who is the domineering, overbearing and controlling personality who everyone walks on egg shells around? They are the ones who create co-dependency. And who are the submissive, manipulated individuals? What about the family members who 'help' the weaker individuals, but in reality their help is enabling because they (the helpers) have a desperate need to be needed?

Let's consider for a moment the neighbors to your left, and recognize a similar order. You'll begin to notice it doesn't matter; a pecking order develops in any group. Think of the classroom to your right, think of the classroom to your left. Think of the business to your right then think of the business to your left. Human drama, 3DL dynamics are virtually the same. The life lesson, the 'earth school', is perfectly designed and set up. 3DL challenges are at our fingertips on a daily, moment-to-moment, second to second basis. Everyday struggles are our 'primer' of opportunities to overcome and for which we could gracefully strive for the 4DL. Some of us think 3DL is the only way to lead a life. Some may never even consider there could be another way. Some never consciously connect with the knowledge that there could be a difference.

Of course there are all the 'in-between' personalities as well who help create and shape the overall dynamics of the group. As a compelling example of family dynamics and, on a grander scale, the survival of life, notice how each individual will move notches up or down in the pecking order as each individual is recognized, heard, valued and understood within the group. Worse, recognize how each individual can and will move notches up or down in a negative manner as well, according to whether they are being misunderstood, devalued or overlooked.

Recognize the pure human drama - clearly a 3DL level. With each life drama, notice the behavior. Notice with each misbehavior exhibited, the more we retreat from entering a 4DL Spirit and the more we choose to remain in our humanness, 3DL. We slip further and further from the Spiritual Being we are as we try to fit into the confines of our family construct. We get all wrapped up in the external energies of fighting, yelling, screaming, sadness, depression… We lose sight of the internal energies of joy, happiness, pleasantness, awe…

———

Possible Miracle Worker Dialog—Context Sensitive

Would you be able to share the following… *'So, looks like you are in the middle of some sort of Spiritual experience. What stops you from being all that you can be? Do you tap into the 95% of the brain you don't use and be the powerful person you were meant to be? What stops you from saying the tough things that need to be said? Looks like you could use a miracle. Address these questions to experience becoming a Miracle Worker. It's not possible to be a Miracle Worker without fearlessly speaking up, standing up, and risking relationships if personal fears and life lessons cloud the moment. Miracle Worker - Heal Thyself!'*

———~~·o·e·ɫ·o·o·ɫ·e·o·~~———

Let's take a look at the different roles being played out within the 'Magic of Chaos' script. In this scene we recognize the Captain; the 'head' of the household who has a thunderous voice. Thunderous voices, what could that mean? Could it be that the Captain is loud and tough because he doesn't know what to do? Being loud could give the illusion of the all knowing, the king of the roost. Or maybe, *'If I'm loud enough I'll scare you into submission and you won't dare ask me questions I don't have the answers to anyway.'* Hmm? Notice how everyone in the room has to get his permission to act upon the solution of writing a simple letter to the Perkins School. Confoundedly, the Captain shares all the different reasons why it seems hopeless to approach the school for the blind.

In our earth 'school' there are a few major life challenges/opportunities we all have experienced. These life experiences, which no one is immune from falling hostage to, we will all experience in some form or another. You may not know these words by definition, but certainly, they are worth exploring so they can be recognized and appropriate tools can then be utilized. These words are: <u>co-dependent</u> and <u>enable</u>; regardless of how the context changes, both words are 3DL.

In this scene, the Captain is the one who creates co-dependency - everyone else is co-dependent; they walk on eggshells around him. Who in your family creates co-dependency? Which members of your family walk on eggshells around maybe someone who acts more like a tyrant or a bully in the house? The other members of the family don't assert their personal power although there is continued dialog. Kate and Aunt Ev encourage writing to the Perkins School for the Blind, and Jimmy brings up a totally different option of placing Helen in an institution, *"Some asylum. It's the kindest thing."* Kate, Aunt Ev and Jimmy in this dialog would be the examples of enablers. They enable, or allow the father figure to express his outrage and indignation, as we get the sense of their hesitancy and their walking on eggshells approach around him.

Where else have you witnessed co-dependencies and enablement? It's not hard to recognize the different players in your neighbor's family dynamics or even to consider the different players within your own family. Sometimes we succumb to being bullied, accepting co-dependency - allowing for the behavior, or maybe we *were* the bully, creating co-dependency. What about the bystander who allowed and enabled the bully to bully? Are there any fearlessly bold individuals out there? How about the bold individual in your home, the individual who called you 'out' on your behavior, the family challenger? Who is the bold fearless individual you most likely condemn, shy away from and have nothing nice to say about because they did call you out? Was this about co-dependency and enablement, or an honest attempt to call you out because someone dared to be the bold one and love you enough to say something? What are the intentions? Ask yourself *what* is the true intention of the situation; *'To hurt me or to build me up?'* Helen could ask: *'Is Miss Annie here to fight with me or for me, to hurt me or build me up? Is she helping me to discover my true potential?'*

What a Miracle Worker Would Share

As the story continues we are introduced to Miss Annie Sullivan, the actual teacher who comes to the Keller family as the result of the letter sent to the Perkins School. Miss Annie is the miracle worker who is the new player, the new bold player being brought into the family. Miss Annie's role is that of the 'family' member who bothers to fearlessly take action and challenge each individual to reach his or her full potential. Much like any child who is mad at a parent and has the courage to say *'No'* to them, Miss Annie says *'No'* loud and clear; over and over, she says *'No.'* Miss Annie is the one who pulled in the reigns of this existing chaos and drama within the Keller family.

Throughout the movie there are several indications that Miss Annie is judgmental, the word is never actually said, but the responses of complaining about Miss Annie's methods, creating power struggles with her efforts, resisting her recommendations, and other non-trusting comments are all indicators that the Keller family certainly felt judged by Miss Annie. Without judging and assessing the family situation, she would not be able to discern how to handle the family or the child. Through her judgments, assessments, and discernments, she nudges Helen and the family into the next level. If Miss Annie's intention is to move the family into a more functional lifestyle: for this, thank goodness for judgment, or better yet we could call her efforts *nudgments*. Miss Annie's intention is to nudge the family into a more functional lifestyle. Thank goodness for nudgments.

Miss Annie was a gift, she was the reason 4DL was introduced into the Keller family, regardless of how anyone felt about her. In the process of introducing a 4DL presence into the Keller's lives it seems much more chaos was created. It looks like more chaos, walks like more chaos, so it must be more chaos. Did Miss Annie create these conflicts within the family dynamics? Or was this just the initial reaction, the power struggle of each family member resisting 4DL? There are family members who don't want to be held responsible or accountable. They don't want to grow up, and these family members don't work toward their full potential. Of course, that is what full potential is all about - it's work. The family resistance was equal in intensity to Helen's resistance or maybe more so, since virtually every member of the family resisted the changes. Resisting change, especially if it means staying stuck in beliefs that don't serve you, is a classic 3DL reaction. Regardless of the conflicts the Keller family experiences initially, we find a certain magic, the real miracles, as the end result. Go Miss Annie!

What would it take to reach your own Spirit? Are you ready to take a good look at yourself? Are you willing to take an inventory of what is going on that's right and what is going on that is not so great? Are you ready to lead a life of more consciousness, awareness and boldness? Are you prepared for the potential chaos required to make the necessary changes in your life in order to progress into a 4DL lifestyle? Are you ready to live fearlessly? Or are you just as resistive to change as the Keller family?

Begin to see the magic of any and all conflict; look for the miracles. Discover your 3DL role in the family dynamics and consider how you will change in order to reach 4DL. Embrace these challenges/opportunities to create the necessary change required for 4DL. What action, what truly fearless action will you take today to make a difference in your environment? You could be your own miracle worker; you could be the hero - if you want. There are those Angels again: *"Ahhhh"*...as you shiver your way to 4DL.

3DL or 4DL is a choice, which lifestyle do you choose?

Fearless– *Synonyms*–dauntless, bold, undaunted, unafraid, confident, intrepid, brave, courageous, undismayed, without fear, unflinching, unshrinking, daring, venturesome

OR

Fearless– *Antonyms*–fearful, cowardly, timorous, daunted, afraid, dismayed, apprehensive, shrinking, terrified

Scene Four

A Plan of Action

The Keller family continues to be frustrated with Helen's behavior. Kate's concern for Helen grows, *"I don't know how to call her back."* Captain Keller finally consents to writing to the Perkins School for the blind.

Aunt Ev: *Helen! My buttons.*
Kate: *Eyes? She wants the doll to have eyes.*
Aunt Ev: *My goodness me. I'm not decent.*
Kate: *She doesn't know better, Aunt Ev. I'll sew 'em on again.*
Aunt Ev: *It's worth a couple of buttons, Kate. Look. This child has more sense than all these men Keller's, if there's ever a way to reach that mind of hers.*
- (baby cries, Helen tips baby sister out of the cradle so she can put her doll in.)
Captain Keller: *Helen!*
Kate: *Helen! Helen! You're not to do such things. How can I make you understand--*
Captain Keller: *Katie!*
Kate: *How can I get it into your head, my darling, my poor--?*
Captain Keller: *Katie, some way of teaching her an iota of discipline has to be--*
Kate: *How can you discipline an afflicted child? Is it her fault?*
Captain Keller: *I didn't say it was her fault.*
Kate: *Then whose? I don't know what to do. How can I teach her, beat her—until she's black and blue?*
Captain Keller: *It's not safe to let her run around loose. Now there must be some way of confinin' her, somehow, so she can't*
Kate: *Where in a cage? She's a growing child - she has to use her limbs!*
Captain Keller: *Answer me one thing. Is it fair to the baby there?*

19

Kate: *Are you willing to put her away?*
Captain Keller: *Now what?*
Kate: *She wants to talk, like -- be like you and me. Every day she slips further away. I don't know how to call her back.*
Aunt Ev: *I do have a mind to write to Boston myself. If that school can't help her, maybe they'll send somebody who can.*
Captain Keller: *I'll write to Perkins, Katie.*

Helen is certainly a naughty girl in this scene. She knocks over everything on dad's desk before he could stop her. Papers fly to the floor, she pulls off Aunt Ev's buttons and tips over her baby sister who is resting in the baby cradle. How bad were your children today? Was there yelling and screaming towards one child over another? How angry were you? Did your blood pressure skyrocket? Did you punish the child? Were you overwhelmed? These would all be typical human 3DL responses. Take a moment to consider all the behaviors your children exhibit that manages to upset you. Just how angry and upset are you with your children today?

Captain Keller is very upset by suggesting: *"Katie, she must be taught some discipline."* Kate responds with: *"How can I teach her? Beat her 'til she's black and blue?"* To which, Captain Keller responds: *"There must be some way of confinin' her."*

Dad's not wrong, something clearly needs to be done with Helen's behavior, but it's Mom who takes the time with Helen to understand what she's trying to communicate. She is more in tune with Helen's Spirit and recognizes that her misbehaviors are just Helen's way of communicating and sharing her frustrations. Helen was trying to get some buttons to represent eyes on her rag doll. Mom understands Helen's frustrations and realizes the child is slipping further and further as she is unable to 'reach' her, to reach her Spirit.

Mom doesn't scold Helen or punish Helen for her misdeeds; there seems to be an understanding of the senselessness of punishment. Mom needs to figure out what Helen is trying to communicate. This overrides the need to be right and punish. What is Helen trying to communicate? What are her needs?

"Meanwhile the desire to express myself grew. The few signs I used became less and less adequate, and my failures to make myself understood were invariably followed by outburst of passion. I felt as if invisible hands were holding me, and I made frantic efforts to free myself.
I struggled - not that struggling helped matters, but the Spirit of resistance was strong within me; I generally broke down in tears in physical exhaustion. If my mother happened to be near I crept into her arms, too miserable even to remember the cause of the tempest. After awhile the need of some means of communication became so urgent that these outbursts occurred daily, sometimes hourly."
-Helen Keller, Story of My Life. p. 12

Mom knows Helen is slipping and doesn't know how to *"call her back."* Mom admits, *"She wants to talk like… be like you and me. Every day she slips further away. I don't know how to call her back."* Kate doesn't know how to reach the essence of Helen; her Spirit. Who knows how to reach the Spirit of any individual? Do you know how to call your child back into their Spirit? Do you know how to reach them at the level they have slipped into? Would you ever have guessed that your precious child who was once a little infant, one you loved so unconditionally could fall, fall so far into their 'human stuff' and you wouldn't know how to reach them? What tools do you have as a parent to call them back?

What parenting skills have we ever been taught? Thinking back on educational curriculum, what life skills were ever taught in the classroom? What venue was designed for students to learn life skills? Maybe a few class meetings, or conflict resolution, mediation, personal growth and development or psychology? Not many, and certainly there were no mandatory classes like those that exist for acquiring a driver's license. There weren't even classes on how to become a good babysitter; even CPR isn't mandatory. With so little resources it's no wonder another day can go by without really addressing the real issues. So begins the belief that *'this is just the way it is'*. Imagine the little to no resources available for the Keller family, not even an internet to surf! How Divinely orchestrated that Miss Annie entered into the Keller's lives when she did.

—⁓⟋⟍—

Possible Miracle Worker Dialog—Context Sensitive

'Tell me about the personal challenge, the life struggles you are experiencing. What action steps could you take? Let's consider a couple of different scenarios where making a decision is difficult to do.

--Let's pretend you are hoping to get the job you just interviewed for, but you are not sure you really want it.

--Let's pretend you really want to get married to your significant other whom you have been with for almost three years.

--Let's pretend you are seriously considering getting into the restaurant business and have just discovered a little café that would be perfect to purchase.

For fun, in your mind's eye, consider you just got the call saying you got the job. What is your first thought, still excited or not so excited?

For fun, in your mind's eye, consider that you were just asked to get married. What is your first thought, excited or not so excited?

For fun, in your mind's eye consider actually signing a business contract for the café. What is your first thought, excited or not so excited?

Roll play in your mind the 'next step' to whatever it is you need to make a decision. See yourself at the job, see yourself as married, see yourself running a café. Are you celebrating while pretending it happened anyway? This is your answer. No need to wait for the dream to come to fruition; pretend it did anyway just to see if this was the dream you actually wanted, or a pipedream?'

—⁓⟋⟍—

There are some clues here. Just like the Keller family, it took frustration and being at their wits end to seek out answers. Phrases like *'This is just the way it is at our house.'* could be a clue that something better is out there. A virtual throwing up of the arms as if to say: *'I give up; I don't know what else to do. I don't want to know.'* Other clues for you to recognize include the frustration of hitting rock bottom, the 3DL, before gaining the courage to admit change could make a difference and taking proactive steps to seek out the options available - 4DL. Save yourself from the headaches, pitfalls and possible financial consequences of these pipedreams by taking a little time to daydream about the dream!

The good news is we can use these various reactions of human drama, of 3DL, as a thermometer or gauge. All chaos, bedlam and human drama could be signs to slow down and consider family options, 4DL. Take these moments to reflect upon the potential it could mean for your life. See the magic of the conflict and the potential for resolution, and not just another hassle-filled day you'd rather avoid and not deal with. The conflict is the gauge; to recognize there is a problem and have the confidence in knowing there is always a solution. Be prepared to fearlessly take action for resolution sake, for the sake of the family. Be open enough to believe something or someone could help make a real difference in your family's lives.

What are your children's needs? How have they tried to communicate, only to be unheard? Who curled up in your lap crying out of frustration and not being understood? Most children don't possess the handicap of being unable to see or hear. Parents don't have to rely on some sort of sign language the child has made up in order to be understood. How blessed we are that our children are healthier and most likely much more capable then Helen… and we still don't take the time to understand them. We are quick to yell, scream, punish, threaten, bribe, or ignore our children. Like Helen, not being heard, validated or understood only escalated the tantrums. Of course it was easier to ignore Helen in the living room until Helen decides being ignored didn't serve her purpose, thus her inappropriate behaviors escalate.

"I do not remember when I first realized that I was different from other people; but I knew it was before my teacher came to me. I had noticed that my mother and my friends did not use signs as I did when they wanted anything done, but talked with their mouths. Sometimes I stood between two persons who were conversing and touched their lips. I could not understand and was vexed.
I moved my lips and gesticulated frantically without result. This made me so angry at times that I kicked and screamed until I was exhausted.
I think I knew when I was naughty, for I knew that it hurt Ella, my nurse, to kick her, and when my fit of temper was over I had the feeling akin to

regret. But I cannot remember any instances in which this feeling prevented me from repeating the naughtiness when I failed to get what I wanted."
-Helen Keller, Story of My Life, p.7

Worse yet, it would be easier to just send her away as Helen's brother Jimmy suggests. *"You really ought to put her away, Father. To some asylum".* A frustrated half brother Jimmy would rather someone else deal with Helen. How many times do we wish we could ship our kids off somewhere for someone else to handle? Don't we exhibit that exact sentiment by sending our children off to school? Don't we hope the teacher will discipline and teach our children manners so we don't have to do it? After all isn't that what the teacher is paid to do, to teach our children? In trying times parents are not considering what their children are trying to communicate or we would see parents handling the child differently. They would take those dedicated moments necessary to understand the child's angst. Taking the time to connect with the child is fast becoming a rusty tool sitting at the bottom of the parent tool box.

How do we know this tool is not being used? Take a moment and think about the kids of today, look in their eyes and see their hurts and pains, see their Spirit struggling on this life plane. How many 'sneaking-around' types of behaviors are they learning in order to cope with their world? Unfortunately this exact type of behavior is being learned earlier and earlier in life. The preliminary introduction to 3DL misbehaviors and shenanigans pushes the innocence right out of a child. The need for escape marks the beginning of misbehaving and experimentation with drugs, alcohol and sex to avoid and numb life challenges that are occurring in one's life. These children don't even want or enjoy going home. Daily household drama makes it difficult for children to want to go home. What is going on in the homes today that children don't want to go home? Do you want to go home? If you don't want to go home, how could your children want to go home? How young these children are with little to no supervision, combined with parents who only throw up their arms exasperated with no solutions and making statements such as *'They're just kids!'* As if this was the grand excuse to allow the child their inappropriate behaviors.

Today's younger children are set up for failure. Go the grocery store, the mall, a dressing room, the beach, church or a restaurant and notice parents who are constantly demanding submission from a child. The child has to adhere to the adult time table. *'Don't do this, don't do that, don't touch that, get over here, I don't want to have to tell you again!'* Listen carefully and you'll hear all the should(s), shouldn't(s), need to, have to, better or else! – Now… here we have a real formula for failure. What's a child to do? Where is the balance, the win/win for the child?

Instead of dragging a child around with you, communicate with the child and let them know what is happening. Invite them to spend the day with you. Let your children know what they can expect when going out. Let them know one of the errands will be boring; it's not a fun kids store and what kind of behavior you expect. Share with the kids what you know about the day so there won't be unexpected surprises. Respectfully, don't you want to know where you are going, who will be there and what you will do? Notice the cooperation you will win from the child when you help them to get on your 'event planners page' for the day. You are the Event Planner in your family, when is the best time to share the event for the day with your children?

As the best Event Planner in the world, how do you win cooperation with adults so the event is deliciously successful and well orchestrated? This takes time, energy and a huge amount of cleverness, ask any Event Planner. Respectfully use these same tools with your children. Create a monthly calendar strategically placed where the kids can see what is happening. Better yet, create a calendar *just* for the kids; have them help you. When they feel a part of the process they will respect the importance of the new change. Empower your children to pencil in their own activities. Be sure to place or hang a pencil right next to the calendar, now they can begin to add their own events to the schedule. A calendar, such a simple idea many families don't even consider.

Family frustrations mount. We all have frustrations, when is it enough? When do we finally admit we don't know what to do and acknowledge with all honesty we could use some help. When do we finally ask; *'What do we do about it?'* What necessary action could we take? What expert is there, who's passionate about their field, has the answers to our questions? Seek solutions.

What a Miracle Worker Would Share

Respectfully see children as individuals who are so very frustrated due to not feeling understood, the lack of parent understanding. Somehow children have to cope in their parent's adult world and have an understanding on a level where it would be impossible for a child to be adult enough or mature enough to understand the adult world. On the other hand, it would seem parents should be the one's able to understand a child and what they are going through, due to the fact that we were all children once with very similar frustrations. We adults insist that children live in our adult world but we don't take the time to visit their world. How could we possibly ask a child to respect us, the adult, when we do not respect the child? It's not in the mirror - there's no mutual reflection.

Take time to respect the child and their needs and watch the child, much like a mirror, reflect back and have an equal amount of respect for you, their parent. You are your children's best model; be amazed about what behaviors they mirror and reflect back to you. Are you role modeling the best behaviors possible for your children to learn? The Universe understands all about the energy surrounding the mirror concept. What you give out, you will get back and this proves true for all areas of life, work, personal relationships, as well as with the children. Be mindful of what messages you are giving and when your child turns around and misbehaves; know your children simply reflected the learned behavior from their best teacher-- you.

How often do we take the time to understand what these misbehaviors are communicating? What would that look like? Maybe a little bit or alot of wide eyed curiosity, leaning in with anticipation, moving or squatting down to their eye level, for the little ones. What is it your child is trying to express to you? See the expression in their eyes. Don't scold or punish the child and their misdeeds. Forgo punishment and being right until you understand the nature of what is going on for the child.

Draw out from the child pointed questions until you notice yourself saying; *"Oh?!"* which means you understand their perspective. *"Oh?!"*- What a simple little word to say, a simple expression of understanding. A word that is both an exclamation and a question expressed at the exact same time. It expresses how awed you are at the explanation and quite simply never saw it from their perspective before, although now you understand. I'm sure you are saying *"Oh?!"* yourself right now! Angels-- *"Ahhh..."*

3DL or 4DL is a choice, which lifestyle do you choose?

Communicate-- *Synonyms*–make known, inform of, announce, apprise of, tell, notify, advise, pass on, convey, disclose, divulge, reveal, relate, bring word, proclaim, state, declare

OR

Communicate-- *Antonyms*–keep secret, hush up, suppress, withhold, hold back, cover up

Scene Five

Risk the Journey

Mr. Michael Anagnos is the Director of the Perkins Institute. He takes Miss Annie to the train station and gives her his last words of wisdom.

Conductor: *Train to New York! And south!*
Mr. Anagnos: *It will no doubt be difficult for you there, Annie, but it has been difficult for you at our school too, hmmm? This is my last time to counsel you, Annie and you do lack some-- and by some I mean all- what? Tact. All talent to bend. To others. And what has saved you on one or occasions at Perkins is that there was nowhere to expel you to. Your eyes hurt?*
Miss Annie: *No my ears.*
Mr. Anagnos: *Nowhere but back to that dreadful place where children learn to be saucy. Annie, I know how unhappy it was there, but that battle is dead and done with. Why not let it stay buried.*
Miss Annie: *I think God must owe me a resurrection*
Mr. Anagnos: *What?*
Miss Annie: *Well, he keeps digging up that battle.*
Mr. Anagnos: *That is not a proper thing to say Annie, be humble.(He hands Miss Annie a gift.) You'll need their affection-- working with this child. A gift with our affection.*
Miss Annie: *Dear Mr Anagnos. I-- Well, What should I say? I'm an ignorant, opinionated girl, and everything I am I owe to you?*
Mr. Anagnos: *That is only half-true, Annie.*
Miss Annie: *Which half?*
Mr. Anagnos (train leaving) Goodbye, goodbye.
Miss Annie: *I won't give them any trouble. I'll be so ladylike they won't notice I've come!*

Notice how we are given a heads up on what kind of personality we can expect Miss Annie to have. *"You do lack some… and by some I mean all - what? Tact. All talent to bend to others."* We've already talked about 'different players' in our life and how we succumb to being bullied, being the bully or allowing the continuation of the behavior and act as a bystander. What about the bold individual in your home? Who is the bold fearless individual you most likely condemn, shy away from and have nothing nice to say about? Who is the family challenger, the truth seeker, the truth-sayer?

In this scene we are introduced to the bold player in Helen's home. *The Miracle Worker* is the bold player within the family and funny enough… the Keller's actually *pay* Miss Annie to be that person! Miss Annie is the new family member to bother, to fearlessly take the necessary action and challenge each individual to reach their potential, the reason for 4DL, regardless of how anyone feels about her.

A favorite comment in this scene from Miss Annie is: *"I won't give them any trouble. I'll be so ladylike they won't notice I've come!"* This is exactly the personality needed to instill change so desperately needed in the Keller household. Who is the person you know who is the change agent so desperately needed in your life? Consider the individual right now who you are having the most difficulty with, who challenges you to your very core? Who is the person in your circle who you blame or stay away from so you can stay in denial about what's really going on in your life? Of course, it's easier to avoid the truth, it's easier not to take action, it's more comfortable to stay in your comfort zone then it is to stretch your belief system, become a better person and make better life choices. Who have you totally dismissed in your life that really had some life changing answers and solutions for you?

Get them back, run to them and tell them how you understand that living life in denial hurts. Taking full responsibility, tell them you would like them back in your life. Ask them to tell you again and again, to teach you how to turn your life around for the better. Most likely this individual is someone you haven't talked to in a long time because you didn't want to 'hear' it. Ironically, that individual is the one who was bold enough to risk the relationship, tell you what you didn't want to hear, for your own good, for which you have totally dismissed them. That special person is the one that is truly concerned for you, that really cares about you; that special person loves you enough to tell you the truth.

Think about the last time someone said '*No!*' to you, and caused you to be hurt and angry because deep down you knew they were right? You decided hanging out in 3DL is more comfortable than risking stepping up to the 4DL, a lifestyle more worthy and conducive to Spiritual development. A lifestyle where you can be your true self, living your full potential. When you are in your Spirit, working all the cylinders of the mind, the body and Spirit, enjoying your potential, then life is full of purpose, life is 4DL.

Only when you are in *your* Spirit can you really serve another in a healthy productive way. Serving others is what makes our Spirit sing; service to others is the best way to be in your 4DL Spirit. Giving to others, sharing with others, watching out for others, touching others and *their* Spirit is at the top of the list of 4DL Spiritual emotions. It gives us chills, as the Angels touch us and we experience goose bumps, then our mind, body and Spirit heals. Remember... this heartfelt feeling, the awe of it all, this is what we strive for as human beings. This is a true celebration that we so very much long for.

There are times in life when we go low; so low and confused we have no recourse but to finally give up the struggle. We become ready for change, we're ready for the better guidance we once dug our heals in and refused. We lose the resistance and are finally ready to accept what makes more sense, to accept better thinking. Finally we want to know; we allow for the new, we allow for 4DL. Notice your particular body posture once you give in to what you really should be doing...this normally includes a huge exhale.

In Helen's case, we will see shortly within the story how the parents realize they are so low, lost and confused about what to do with their little girl. It is as if they are tired of giving Helen fish; they are now ready to explore ways of discovering some options for teaching her *how* to fish. Finally, they allow for the 'bold Miss Annie' to teach her, work with her and if nothing else, 'snap' some sense of better behavior into Helen. Thus, thrusting Helen into 4DL, which of course Helen didn't want or like either, but it was good for her, and the right thing to do. But what a tug of war! You've probably noticed that similar tug of war experience when you don't listen to the mind, body, Spirit connection. With such a tug of life when we resist 4DL, we must count on Divine Interventions to prevail.

My guess is there is someone in your life who loves you enough to play tug of life as they introduce you to a 4DL. But instead of honoring the knowledge and wisdom, you took your bat and ball away to find someone else who would continue to play a 3DL game. Someone to help you stay stuck in the 3DL.

It's not hard to find individuals who will enable you. After all, they think they are your friends and are busy helping you. You think they are your friends - helping you. This is not a healthy friend. These individuals confuse *helping* with *enabling*. Often we prefer to be enabled, in a sense we enjoy being pitied, babied and taken care of. We like these unhealthy people around us. They don't ask anything of us, they only give and give, to us. They want to rescue the poor down and out helpless, hopeless victim. Who doesn't want that? Truth is - what a great way to be distracted from your Spirit, from potential and to remain in denial. All this attention keeps us from becoming pure potential, albeit inappropriate attention.

Possible Miracle Worker Dialog-- Context Sensitive

Have you ever found yourself being that unhealthy friend, wanting to rescue the poor down and out helpless, hopeless victim? We are ready to hand out any 'bailout' they need. Many times we enable the situation when we thought we were actually helping them. Here are some phrases to keep in your back pocket to empower and encourage a friend instead of enabling them -

-*'You are a clever person, you will do well.'*
-*'I trust your judgment. Enjoy the adventure.'*

-*'I'm sure you will handle everything just fine.'*
-*'Your enthusiasm tells me you are very excited about your new adventure.'*

―――― ᴍ•ᴏᴇ•ᴏᴏ•ᴇ•ᴏ•ᴍ ――――

What a Miracle Worker Would Share

Think about one person in your life who was trying to shed some light on you and who you totally rejected because you didn't want to 'hear' it, you didn't want to know. Take a minute to evaluate whether or not that loving individual was trying to hurt you *or* raise you up. Was that individual nudging you or judging you? Be as honest as you can and admit you didn't really want to know, you didn't want to hear it. Life is so much easier to handle when you can blame a fearless individual who only wanted the best for you.

A Miracle Worker would share with you, again and again, to realize how your mind was only trying to fool your heart. Go to that person, now, today. Honor that wisdom, ask them to come back into your life and teach you how to raise your standards, to have some sense of decorum, to build a moral compass. Have them teach you how to listen to your Spirit as you learn to shift your beliefs from 3DL to 4DL. Most important of all, recognize that, ultimately, you want to be the best you can be - always! You are just afraid. You are afraid of the power that you are, you are afraid of the power you have. Acknowledge instead that you are happy and willing to receive loving, constructive criticism. Even when it doesn't feel loving!

These new tools that help raise your standard, your vibration, will most definitely be tools you'll need to teach your children one day. This is especially true if you want them to be the best they can be, and hopefully even better than you. What a gift to yourself, to your children and to the Universe; making sure your children are better, smarter, wiser than you. A Miracle Worker would encourage that!

Awaken to the process of life, at least the part called the circle of life; the next generation. What is the next generation *really* all about? We grow the next generation, and then we mold them. Mold them for what exactly? We teach them from pre-school and up, to do what? What is the next generation here for? What is their purpose? Do we teach them everything we know and then get offended when they may end up knowing more than us? Some call this the generation gap.

Are we clear about the succession of generations? We may recognize children are here to learn from us. Success happens when our children then become our teachers and help expand the worldview further. We can raise our own conscious awareness and embrace children to awaken in us what is missing. In turn *they* prepare *their* children for further worldviews. Great success occurs when *our* children become capable, autonomous and smarter than *us*.

Children are not afraid to tap into their thoughts, feelings and intuition. They have an innate sense of what is right, what is wrong, what is incomplete and what is missing. If given permission, they can awaken in us what is missing, what is lost. If given the freedom and opportunity they could explore with us the areas long forgotten by the elder generations.

Of course, this would mean putting aside our personal fears and agendas. We would need to awaken to what might initially feel like criticism and humiliation. Can we suspend judgment and not be offended by their mind, body and Spiritual growth; the same growth we currently long for?

Be secure in yourself. Take the brakes off and open up to new thoughts and ideas. Consider seeing children as equals. Equal enough to give them the time to express their heartfelt thoughts, just like you would a good friend sitting over a cup of coffee. Learn to draw out from the child their particular passions and beliefs. Ask questions. Ask pointed questions. Why are they here? What are the gifts they have to give? How will they serve? Be prepared to be amazed, showered with new and innovative ideas. Honor the wisdom, and support their future, their hopes and their dreams.

It is through this process that you are beginning to break the dysfunctional 3DL cycle within your family. What you have learned from growing up in your former 3DL family will now be substituted for a 4DL lifestyle. You experience life differently because what was once passed down from generation to generation stops with you. This is the ultimate in making the conscious connection, this is transformation, this is 4DL, and this is a choice. I can hear those Angels again! *"Ahhhh..."*

3DL or 4DL is a choice, which lifestyle do you choose?

Bold–   *Synonyms–*brave, courageous, valiant, unafraid, fearless, heroic, unshrinking, daring, creative, adventuresome, daredevil, imaginative

OR

Bold–   *Antonyms–*cowardly, fainthearted, fearful, shrinking, flinching

Scene Six

Withstanding Judgment

Miss Annie Arrives!

Conductor: *Tuscumbia! Tuscumbia*
Brother Jimmy: *Miss Sullivan?*
Miss Annie: *Here, at last. I've been on trains so many days. I thought the trains must be backing up every time I dozed off.*
Brother Jimmy: *I'm James Keller.*
Miss Annie: *James? I had a brother Jimmy. Are you Helen's?*
Brother Jimmy: *I'm only half her brother. You're to be her governess?*
Miss Annie: *Well, try!*
Brother Jimmy: *You look like half a governess. You have a trunk, Miss Sullivan?*
Miss Annie: *Yes.*
Brother Jimmy: *Mrs. Keller. (pointing to the carriage)*
Kate: *We've met every train for two days*
Miss Annie: *You didn't bring Helen? I was hoping you would.*
Kate: *No, she's home.*
Miss Annie: *You live far from town, Mrs. Keller?*
Kate: *Only a mile.*
Miss Annie: *Well, I suppose I could wait one more mile. But don't be surprised if I get out and push the horse.*
Kate: *There's been such a bustle preparing your room, she expects someone.*
Captain Keller: *Welcome to Ivy Green, Miss Sullivan.*
Kate: *My husband, Miss Annie. Captain Keller.*
Miss Annie: *Captain, how do you do?*
Captain Keller: *Pleasure to see you, at last. I trust you had an agreeable journey.*

Miss Annie: *Oh, I had several.*

Brother Jimmy: *Where do you want the trunk, father?*

Captain Keller: *Where Miss Sullivan can get at it, I imagine...*

Miss Annie: *Yes, please. Where's Helen?*

Captain Keller: *And the suitcase.*

Miss Annie: *I'll take that. I've got something for Helen. When do I see her?*

Kate: *There. There's Helen. (Miss Annie walks toward Helen)*

Captain Keller: *Katie... Sh. She's very rough.*

Kate: *I like her, Cap'n.*

Captain Keller: *How old is she?*

Kate: *Well, she's not in her teens, you know.*

Captain Keller: *Why does she wear those glasses? I like to see a person's eyes when I talk to 'em.*

Kate: *For the sun. She was blind.*

Captain Keller: *Blind?*

Kate: *She had nine operations on her eyes. One just before she left.*

Captain Keller: *Blind? Good heavens! They expect one blind child to teach another? How long did she teach there?*

Kate: *She was a pupil.*

Captain Keller: *This is her first position?*

Kate: *She was Valedictorian.*

Every day we meet new people. Be it a new neighbor, a new co-worker, a new friend. It only takes a matter of minutes before we size them up, collect evidence and decide how we feel about them and how to treat them. It could be we don't like the way they talk, what they are wearing, or we think their shoes are from some discount store. Or we might discover we don't like their name because we knew someone with that same name and they were unfriendly. Or maybe they have a similar pair of glasses and a beard, which reminds you of your grandfather and you never got along with your grandfather. The big surprise would be to give them the time of day and realize you actually liked them; 4DL. You may be amazed with how much you actually have in common if given the chance.

Many would call the above comments *judgmental*. Some judge the fact that you judged! Be aware of those accusing you of judging. Usually this is someone who is pointing the finger claiming that somehow you are being inappropriate for 'judging'. This is called a distraction, noise, to get the heat off of them and back onto you. Be glad that you judge. Thank goodness you judge, judging helps you discern right from wrong, good from bad, up from down, good friends from not so good friends.

What we may need to consider is whether or not our judgment is 3DL judgment or 4DL 'nudgment'? 3DL judgment would be all tied up as human drama, ego-based with a need to put someone down in order to feel better than them. 4DL nudgment is based on a Spiritual assessment. The ability to discern what step to take next, what action is needed to keep yourself or someone you know and love safe. 4DL nudgment comes from the heart, from love for another rather than a selfish love for self. Only you can determine whether you are coming from a human dramatic point of view or a Spiritual one. Only you can determine your own intention. Ask yourself, what is your intention with this individual? What are you doing? With all honesty reel your mind in; stop it from running 3DL amok.

So something doesn't seem quite right about them, check it out, investigate, and take the necessary steps to find out. It is quite possible the person really reminds you of that part of you that you don't particularly like about yourself, or the person reminds you about that part of you that you wish you were more like. Back off a bit, at least long enough to risk getting close and be amazed how you actually get along; discover this bonus. They have something to teach you, something you want to know, or something you have been interested in learning about. You won't know what that 'thing' is until you get to know them better.

In Helen's case, the Kellers really wanted what Miss Annie had. They often waffled between giving her a chance and being confused about her. They judged with total 3DL beliefs until a Divine intervention forced them to drop the judgment and recognize the nudgment to realize Miss Annie was the 4DL teacher they needed. As the story continues we will notice how Miss Annie's 4DL beliefs help Mr. and Mrs. Keller, and even brother Jimmy as they begin to reach their own 4DL potential.

Who have you judged recently? Maybe you judged someone new, a new business acquaintance, a new idea, or maybe a new opportunity? How did this possibly ruin some great opportunities for you and your family? Ask questions, and remove all doubt, but don't put the brakes on until you have given them a chance. How much easier life could have been for Miss Annie and for the Kellers as well if they could have judged Miss Annie using a 4DL belief system from the very beginning of their introduction? Lucky for Helen that Mom took off the brakes, even if Dad and Brother Jimmy continued to squeal with the breaks on!

Possible Miracle Worker Dialog - Context Sensitive

Kate is being blasted by Captain Keller and even Miss Annie is not being treated so nicely by Jimmy. The Captain asks one question right after another, like a machine gun. Who in your life uses interrogation with you? Identify that person by name. You can always count on this person to act this way especially when there is confusion, doubt and possible misunderstanding. You may not be experiencing the confusion, but they do. Certainly this recognition helps you to realize their gruffness is not about you - at all!

Take a minute and role play in your mind the next possible conversation you could have. Count on a new opportunity to present itself, a healing is forthcoming. Place these phrases in your back pocket, ready to use at any moment. Choose according to the context of the situation.

-*'I can see you have some concerns.'*
-*'You seem to have a lot of questions.'*
-*'I would be happy to answer all of your questions.'*
-*'You have certainly put me on the spot; I will not answer your questions.'*
-*'I want to hear everything you have to say and then I will share with you.'*
-*'I can see you are anxious. How can you ask me so that I would be willing to co-operate?'*

Some interesting facts about Miss Annie Sullivan

"Miss Anne Mansfield Sullivan was born in Springfield Massachusetts. Very early in her life she became almost totally blind, and she entered the

Perkins Institution on October 7, 1880, when she was fourteen years old. Later, her sight was partially restored."

Story of My Life. P.248

"In 1886 she graduated from the Perkins Institution. When Captain Keller applied to the director for a teacher, Mr. Anagnos recommended her. The only time she had to prepare herself for the work with her pupil was from August 1886, when Captain Keller wrote, to February, 1887. During this time she read Dr. Howe's reports. She was further aided by the fact that during the six years of her school life she had lived in the house with Laura Bridgeman. It was Dr. Howe who, by his work with Laura Bridgeman, made Miss Sullivan's work possible; but it was Miss Sullivan who discovered the way to teach language to the deaf-blind."

Story of My Life. p.249

"It must be remembered that Miss Sullivan had to solve her problems unaided by previous experience or the assistance of any other teacher."

Story of My Life. p.249

What a Miracle Worker Would Share

Every day in life we will experience new experiences, we will meet new people, be exposed to new opportunities and challenges. Every day we can make a new choice, create new opportunities and be open to the potential of the day. We can wake up each morning asking: *'How will I be responsible for my day? What will I create? What new experience will happen today? Who have I judged today, or what have I judged that could have gotten in the way of synchronicity, coincidences, or serendipity?'*

All of this is a choice, your choice. A choice to allow a perfect alignment created by the Universe to be part of our lives or not. A choice which can become a bit skewed, if we allow for fears, judgments and doubts to be the action choice of the day. Judge your children, what are they communicating? Judge those at work, are they trying to manipulate? Judge your own judgments. Take time to notice a 3DL or 4DL choice. Bother to take the time to discern your life and discern new choices based on sound judgment grounded in a 4DL.

This book can unleash the many tools available in your own tool box, especially the ones that are rusty and dusty at the bottom. But what good are they if they aren't used? It's most likely that the tools that aren't being used, the rusty dusty tools at the bottom of the tool box, are those in which you might need some reminders and new instruction on how to fine tune their use. Pick them up, dust them off, touch them, and develop a fondness for them, embrace them. Find a way to become comfortable with all the endless tools and their possibilities in the tool box. Play with them, every shape, and every size, find a comfort level. Discover all that they can do. A hair clip can fix the weed wacker or even a plastic cigarette lighter can open a bottle of beer! Try it!

Your children depend on you to guide them and show them the way - everything a child requires to stay safe. Teach them and equip them with all the tools you know about, they will need them in their lives for the challenges and life lessons that are sure to be theirs in earth school. What are the best tools to build their self-esteem? What tools will work best to create independent individuals ready to take on their world, their lives, and their challenges/opportunities ethically? How will you create autonomous children so their life choices and decisions are based from within themselves and not outside of themselves, begging for approval or permission? How will you encourage your children to be *better* than you so they will be *better off* than you? Wherever you leave off in this life time, at whatever point you give up in this life time, how will your children carry on from the place you left off? How will they carry on and improve the next generation?

Why wouldn't we do this for our children? You may want to search your heart and see your own 3DL issues which could then leave your children wanting and needy. Check in with your own self-esteem, or perhaps more correctly, your lack of self-esteem, which would allow you to keep your children in lack. Remember the mirror work earlier, where you lack, your children will lack. This may require a need to heal yourself first of your own inadequacies and self doubts. Role model for your children the joy of embracing learning everything about yourself and everything it may take to build yourself up. Teach them to be curious and to ask questions in order to have the most glorious and intimate relationship with themselves. Have them watch your body language; one of leaning in, of wide eyed excitement in learning a new piece about yourself. This is not the time to be shy…another choice.

The word 'everything' in this context means the good and the not so good. Your children will acquire the same joy of learning everything there is about themselves, just as you had the joy of learning everything about *yourself.* They will exhibit the same moral soundness, the same ethics as you. There's that mirror again, and isn't this the better reflection you would want to see for yourself and your children? Hold yourself accountable and responsible for the children of tomorrow, the future depends on it. My children depend on it. I thank you for parenting, for speaking up to your children by learning all the tools you can learn about. Now my children have healthy partners to pick from, a safer more productive world to live in. The 3DL dysfunctional home life cycle begins to break down. Break the dysfunctional cycle in your family. I can hear the choir of Angels *"Ahhhh…"*

3DL or 4DL is a choice, which lifestyle do you choose?

Ethical– *Synonyms*–moral, decent, virtuous, honorable, upright, proper, fitting, correct, just, fair, aboveboard, straightforward, open

OR

Ethical– *Antonyms*–underhanded, shady, improper, unfair, low-down, crooked, unbecoming, unseemly, immoral, indecent

Scene Seven

Attention Seeking

In this section, there are three different scenes involving Brother Jimmy to illustrate his role and how he is treated by the family.

Brother Jimmy: *I'm James Keller.*
Miss Annie: *James? I had a brother Jimmy. Are you Helen's?*
Brother Jimmy: *I'm only half her brother. You're to be her governess?*
Miss Annie: *Well, try.*
Brother Jimmy: *You look like half a governess. You have a trunk, Miss Sullivan?*

The point of sharing the three different scenes is to recognize how the same personal life pattern repeats over and over. Your personal pattern repeats over and over, and my pattern repeats over and over until we consciously connect and make a different choice about how to handle the situation, thus changing the pattern.

Poor Jimmy, with all the attention Helen receives for her afflictions; Jimmy is left out, hardly heard and often overlooked. In this text he refers to himself as: *"…only half her brother."* Of course Helen would be getting the majority of the attention; she is, after all, the needy child in the family with the most challenges. She's what would be called the squeaky wheel, and we all know about squeaky wheels. Who is the squeaky wheel in your family? Who needs most of the attention due to illness? Or maybe someone in your family has an addiction the family enables. Or it could be a needy sibling in trouble with the law that everyone enables and gives too much attention to out of pity and over compensation. Which family member has had to give up their life, a fair amount of attention, and take a back seat due to an unhealthy family environment perpetuated by the fact that most individuals mistake 'helping' someone with 'enabling' someone?

When is helping overstepping and infringing on the truth of pure enablement? Helping is no longer helpful when the help doesn't foster or develop independence. In that case, helping is now enabling. Enablement is when we spend so much time helping another we lose focus on the self. Enablement is when we can't take the time to create our own lives because we're too busy creating someone else's life. Enablement is when we are the Spiritual essence of another and not our own Spiritual self; we've given up our own lives, our own dreams, our own aspirations, our own Spirit. Enablement looks and feels like a noble thing to do... so giving, so selfless. Don't be fooled, don't deny the truth of the unhealthy 3DL need to be needed, look good, or to have purpose.

I can assure you, you have purpose. It looks a little different than the current misguided belief. Your purpose is your own personal life to experience, to lead. I can also assure you, if you don't lead with passion towards personal potential then Divine interventions are coming your way. Like a cosmic two by four, the Universe has specially designed wrenches to disturb and distract your enabling tendencies. The Universe will create situations for you to recognize that 3DL helping is really enabling. The purpose of your life is to *live* your life, discover your purpose, honor yourself, and honor your Spirit. Nothing will be right in your World until you begin in earnest your own personal life journey. Ducks won't line up, planets won't be in line, nothing will fall into place and life will be a constant struggle. You will feel like you are moving two steps forward only to fall three steps back. Take an inventory of what your life is really about; is it your life by your design or are you living someone else's life with their whims, fantasies and neediness?

When families become tired of being tired, are at their wits end and just don't know what to do, an intervention of some sort is played out. It may be a natural consequence or a Divine intervention, or it may be a family planned-out intervention. Sometimes you can't wait for the Divine intervention; sometimes you may have to ask what could be done, how do we intervene now? This is especially true if you spot it recognizing there is something you could do, take action. What action can we take now to bring the bottom up? For example, if a family member is on drugs or alcohol, you wouldn't want to wait for them to reach their bottom and possibly lose them for life? A professional, mediated intervention is right at the top of the list of the most loving and caring things any one could do for another. A concentrated family effort to shift an unhealthy 3DL to an empowering 4DL, now that's love! No doubt, chaos and confusion in full throttle pushing through defiance, now who wouldn't want to be loved like that?

In Helen's case the Kellers brought the bottom up, they took the responsibility and intervened inviting Miss Annie into the fray. Kate knew Helen was slipping and feared she wouldn't know how to get her back. Who do you know who is slipping to a dangerously low point? It doesn't have to be about alcohol or drugs. It could be about anorexia, bulimia, co-dependency, and enablement or in Helen's case deafness and blindness. Who are you losing? Who is stuck in 3DL, lost and confused and not living their full life potential? Will you wait for the bottom for the fall out and risk losing them forever or will you be part of a grander plan and participate in a family planned well thought out intervention today?

Further into the scene the following dialog is played out:

Brother Jimmy: *You really ought to put her away, Father.*
Captain Keller: *What?*
Brother Jimmy: *Some asylum. It's the kindest thing.*
Kate: *She is your sister, James.*
Brother Jimmy: *Half-sister and half... mentally defective. She can't keep herself clean. It's not pleasant to see her about.*
Kate: *Do you dare complain of what you can see?*

Clearly Jimmy is at his wits end also. Here we see his suggestion about an asylum to put Helen away. Jimmy feels this is the *"kindest thing"*. As drastic as that sounds to us I'm sure, in the day, there weren't too many options available for the deaf and blind. Certainly there weren't any computers to surf on the internet to discover some options. Of course

Jimmy's suggestions don't sit well with Kate. As a mom, she knows Helen has more potential than Jimmy or the rest of the family may actually realize. Instinctively, it's usually mommies who have their pulse on the family situation and realize more than other family members.

Captain Keller: *A houseful of grown-ups can't cope with Helen. How can a half-blind Yankee schoolgirl manage?*
Brother Jimmy: *Great improvement. Now we have two of them.*
Kate: *You be quiet.*
Brother Jimmy: *I was agreeing with you.*
Kate: *You talk too much.*
Brother Jimmy: *Nothing I say is right.*
Kate: *Why say anything?*

Another example of Jimmy being misunderstood and overlooked regardless of the appropriate or inappropriate statements he makes. Who are the co-dependent family members? The clues are in the sentence asking: *'Which family member has had to give up their life, a fair amount of attention and take a back seat?'* There are usually one or two family members who squeak so loudly the other family members fear leading a self-fulfilled life. Their lives are so preoccupied and consumed with the household drama. The same was true in Helen's home and it was Jimmy always being referred to as "Brother Jimmy" who was a victim of the family dynamics. Notice it was Jimmy who disciplined Helen the most and therefore was most likely looked upon as the one who didn't understand, didn't have enough sympathy or pity for Helen. After all Jimmy most certainly wasn't the professional conflict resolution/mediator many families need to overcome or master family challenges/opportunities.

Possible Miracle Worker Dialog: Context Sensitive

We never know exactly why we say the things we say, when we say them, especially hurtful things. We never know why others say hurtful things. Believe for now that the 'why' is not what is important. How to respond, is what is important. Eighty to eighty-five percent of interpersonal communication is done through body language; we don't even need words. What if we could perfect a dialog with a love look? A look that accepts an individual in the moment of their confusion, doubt and frustrations as if to say... *'How cute are you...you are so in your stuff.'* Miracle Workers have this look - you'll need to practice.

What a Miracle Worker Would Share

Recognize who in your family is the squeaky wheel and how this individual or individuals are monopolizing family time and energy. Who has given up their lives in order to 'help'? Who has been neglected in the family? Each of the individuals who play these roles in your family is not healthy either. They need tools to cope with the unhealthy family dynamics. True healing comes when they are able to live their own lives, and not to sacrifice their life and enable therefore perpetuating a bad situation. It seems Brother Jimmy gets into trouble for speaking up and he gets into trouble for not speaking at all.

Of course, be warned about helping another vs. enabling another. Be sure your service is empowering. Teach others to help themselves, teach others to fish instead of performing the type of service which is enabling by overdoing for others, by handing out fish after fish. Realize if you start giving fish you will always give out fish; you will always rescue the situation and the situation will always need to be rescued. If, on the other hand, you teach others to fish, then you know they can feed themselves. If you teach your child to fish, encouraging independence is a true indication of your healthy understanding which creates self-sufficiency and autonomously-centered children. This independence is a sign of a healthy child turned adult who will be accountable and responsible for their own lives. These children won't expect handouts and bailout. This is the mark of a parent job well done. Who will be the intervention expert, professional or not, with the resources necessary to relieve the family dysfunction in your home? Who will be your Miracle Worker? Learn to love them when many times you want to hate them, because they were right and you know it! Angels? *"Ahhhh..."*

3DL or 4DL is a choice, which lifestyle do you choose?

Attention–   *Synonyms*–heed, regard, notice, mind, concern, consider, observe, alertness, thought

OR

Attention–   *Antonyms*–disregard, neglect, negligence, thoughtlessness, carelessness

Scene Eight

Assessing Potential

March 6, 1887 *"She helped me unpack my trunk when it came, and was delighted when she found the doll the little girls sent her. (Miss Annie is referring to the girls at the Perkins School) I thought it a good opportunity to teach her first word. I spelled d-o-l-l..."*
Story of My Life, Annie Sullivan. P.252

Miss Annie: All the trouble I went to and that's how I look? Oh, no, not the drawers. (doll makes sound) All right, Miss O'Sullivan. Let's begin with doll. D...O...L...L. Doll.
Brother Jimmy: You spell pretty well. Finding out if she's ticklish? She is. What is it, a game?
Miss Annie: An alphabet.
Brother Jimmy: Alphabet?
Miss Annie: For the deaf. How bright she is.
Brother Jimmy: You think she knows what she's doing? She's a monkey. She imitates everything.
Miss Annie: Yes, she's a bright little monkey, all right.
Brother Jimmy: She wants her doll back.
Miss Annie: When she spells it.
Brother Jimmy: Spell, she doesn't know the thing has a name.
Miss Annie: Of course not. Who expects her to now? All I want is her fingers to learn the letters.
Brother Jimmy: Won't mean anything to her. She doesn't like that alphabet. You invent it yourself?
Miss Annie: Spanish monks under a vow of silence, which I wish you'd take.

The Keller family and especially Helen have met their match and Miss Annie is up for the challenge. Right away Miss Annie discovers how smart and clever Helen is. She sees Helen's potential even if Brother Jimmy belittles Helen's intelligence. Miss Annie views Helen in a different light and does not buy into the disbeliefs Brother Jimmy expresses. Instead, Miss Annie hangs onto her discoveries about Helen and responds with *"Yes, she's a bright little monkey, all right."*

March 11, 1887 *"I think, however, she will learn quickly enough by and by. As I have said before, she is wonderfully bright and active and as quick as lightning in her movements."*
Story of My Life, Annie Sullivan. P.259

You'll notice in the next scene that Miss Annie is prepared to take the time with Helen until she spells 'doll'. Brother Jimmy doesn't believe Helen will be able to spell 'doll' in this sign language stuff and again, Miss Annie sticks to her beliefs and will wait Helen out. Miss Annie doesn't have much to work with since Helen can neither hear nor see so she must virtually hang tangible items, like the doll, over Helen's head. Miss Annie needs to find out what is most important to Helen and work with those items as a tool to reach her. In this case a piece of cake. Miss Annie knows the hand signs she repeats over and over and over ad nauseum, will be those words that have to do with items Helen is familiar with or the items that Helen has around her most often. It is in this constant repeating of these beloved few items that Helen will eventually connect and be able to attach the hand sign to the item.

Miss Annie is okay with Helen repeating the hand spelling like a monkey. She understands that Helen doesn't know what it means - for now. Miss Annie knows and trusts or at the very least hopes that the seeds she plants with Helen will one day grow and blossom. She has one job; to reach Helen where no one has been able to reach her. Miss Annie can see through to Helen's intelligence and knows she's a bright little girl. Through observations Miss Annie recognizes Helen has already created her own versions of signing to communicate. Signs only she understands the meaning and created out of pure survival need. On one observation, Miss Annie witnesses Helen playing with the cooks little girl, Martha Washington. Helen wins Martha over and is even able to manipulate her little playmate. It is exactly these already learned skills that Miss Annie recognizes as tools she can work and grow with.

> *"In those days a little colored girl, Martha Washington, the child of our cook, and Belle, an old setter and a great hunter in her day, were my constant companions.*
> *Martha Washington understood my signs and I seldom had any difficulty in making her do just as I wished. It pleased me to domineer over her, and she generally submitted to my tyranny rather than risk a hand-to-hand encounter. I was strong, active, and indifferent to consequences. I knew my own mind well enough and always had my own way, even if I had to fight tooth and nail for it."*
> **Helen Keller, The Story of My Life p.7.**

Odds have it you are the Miss Annie in someone's life. Possibly a child, since you are reading this book possibly looking for some practical, miracle worker life skill tools. You may have already realized the child needs more. You want the best for this child. It's time to explore what's 'best' regardless of the child's handicap. It is time to wake up your sleeping child. It is time to force the child to look, to champion the will, to become aware and prepare for the game of life.

Possible Miracle Worker Dialog: Context Sensitive

'Wake up sleepy head, today is the day. It is time to take a more active role in your own life. It's time for me to let go, cut the apron string and let you experience life as the Universe has planned. It is time for you to learn to be self-sufficient, self reliant, autonomous. I'm here to support you in any and every way you need, but I'm no longer here to enable you. I love you enough to do this for you.'

Miracle Worker Self Talk-- Every day, I will ask myself; *'What one activity or enabling am I doing for the child that they could really be doing for themselves?'* Every day I will ask myself; *'What one thing do I need to do so that I can make room for the child to grow and develop that encourages autonomy?'* Maybe more importantly I will ask myself; *'What one thing do I need to do to better myself to grow and develop my life instead of growing and developing theirs? What one thing do I need to do so I can let go and let the child be personally responsible for their own life? I understand this frees up my time so I can create the life the Universe has in store for me too?'* (Remember the age of the child is of no importance, this applies to ALL children).

———

Helen's parents realized Helen was ready for more in her life and just didn't know how to accomplish the next step. As concerned parents, Mr. and Mrs. Keller want the best for Helen. It was time to explore what 'best' would look like for someone like Helen, someone who is deaf and blind. The parents may not like or even understand the different strategies that could be available for Helen. Certainly the parents misunderstood the unconventional approach which Miss Annie seemed to think was necessary considering Helen's handicaps. Miss Annie also knows Helen is at the mental age and stage she's at because the parents are quite frankly - stuck. Up to this point in Helen's life, this is as far as the parents have been able to work with Helen. If Miss Annie is to make a serious impact on Helen, the approach would have to be different from what the parents were already doing. It was time for a different approach and a different strategy, even the misunderstood unconventional ones.

What a Miracle Worker Would Share

Miss Annie is strong in her convictions. She knows what she's looking for while she tests and observes Helen. Miss Annie's past personal experience with blindness also helps her to stand strong in her convictions to do what she feels is right. Miss Annie is different and unconventional, she can hang tough and trusts the decisions she makes. There will be times when you need to walk away from the doubting Thomas, the naysayers. Or just as Miss Annie did with Brother Jimmy, closing the door on him after saying, *"Spanish monks under a vow of silence, which I wish you'd take."* Hopefully, there will be a time in your life when you will decide to invite certain individuals who are responding from a 3DL position, to leave your presence so you can remain strong in your 4DL beliefs.

Do you know where you are going? Do you know what the next step is? Even if you don't know the exact end result, can you take the next necessary step? You may not know what you want exactly, but you certainly know what you don't want. Do you take the necessary steps daily? Odds have it there is someone in your life that worries about you, someone who wants the 'best' for you. They know you aren't taking your next step. There is that person in the pecking order who knows you aren't living up to your true potential. Who have you escaped from? Who is that someone who rocks your world and turns things upside down, demanding certain more appropriate life responses from you? Someone who understands clearly that tantrums and pity tactics don't work on them? Who is that very special someone in your life who challenges you and like a mirror puts the lesson before you? Who expects you to get back into the game of life? Angels! *"Ahhhh!"*

3DL or 4DL is a choice, which lifestyle do you choose?

Different– *Synonyms–*unlike, dissimilar, not identical, not alike, distinct, divergent, contrasting, distinct, individual

OR

Different– *Antonyms–*identical, alike, same, similar, like, common, usual, typical, conventional.

Scene Nine

The Intention of the Universe

In this scene, Miss Annie continues to work with Helen on the sign language for d-o-l-l. Helen's frustrations had her leaving Miss Annie's room, locking the door behind her. Chaos unfolds...

Miss Annie: Yes... Yes! C... A...K... E. Yes. You do as my fingers do. Never mind what it means. Now... D...O... L... L. Think it over. Imitate now. Understand later. End of the first les---Ow! Oh, you little wretch. Nobody's taught you any manners.(Helen hits Miss Annie with the doll and locks Miss Annie in the room and takes the key.) - Helen! Helen! Helen, let me out of--. Don't worry, they'll find you. You're not lost. Only out of place. And toothless!

Captain Keller: Where's Miss Sullivan?

Brother Jimmy: Locked in her room.

Captain Keller: Locked in her...?

Brother Jimmy: Helen locked her in and took the key.

Kate: And you sit here and say nothing?

Brother Jimmy: Everyone's been telling me not to say anything.

Kate: Viney, look out front for Helen.

Captain Keller: She's out by the pump!

Captain Keller: Miss Sullivan.

Miss Annie: Yes, Captain Keller.

Captain Keller: Is there no key on your side?

Miss Annie: If there were a key, I wouldn't be in here. Helen took it. The only thing on my side is me.

Captain Keller: Not in the house ten minutes. I don't see how you managed it.

Miss Annie: And even I'm not on my side.

Captain Keller: Viney!

Viney: *Yes, sir, Captain Keller?*
Captain Keller: *Viney! Put that meat back in the oven!*
Kate: *She has no key.*
Captain Keller: *Nonsense, she must have the key. Have you searched in her pockets?*
Kate: *Yes. She doesn't have it. (Jimmy appears carrying a ladder.)*
Captain Keller: *Katie, she must have the key. Take that ladder back!*
Brother Jimmy: *Certainly.*

Miss Annie continues to collect evidence about how clever and cunning Helen is. How clever and cunning Helen is indeed to lock Miss Annie in her room *and* take the key. Here is a child who recognizes this new someone; her teacher who dares to challenge her. This new someone is rocking Helen's world, turning things upside down, demanding certain, more appropriate and better behavioral responses. Tantrums don't work with this new person; pity doesn't work with this new person. Tantrums and pity used to work. Who wouldn't want to leave an environment like that and escape someone who puts the lesson right in your face over and over, each day?

This scene is a very symbolic scene for all families. Who was locked out of your life and out of your family's lives, the one who could have made the difference? Here you are, a child (from 7 to 70, age doesn't matter) who recognizes someone who dares to challenge you, someone who is rocking your world, turning things upside down, demanding certain, appropriate responses. You find that tantrums don't work with your own 'Miss Annie' person, pity doesn't work with your 'Miss Annie' person either. Who challenges you and who do you run from? Is this person the one who could make the difference in your world? How clever you are to lock the 'Miss Annie' of your world in her room *and* take the key. Who wouldn't want to leave an environment like that and escape? Your clue is in recognizing who you dismissed, most likely in anger and in a huff, and whom you truly need to invite back into your world.

Let's have another look at Brother Jimmy. In the Keller family, not unlike your own family, each member of the family has recognizable response patterns. You can count on each family member responding the same way according to the family pecking order. Throughout the movie we see Brother Jimmy as exhibiting the same behavior pattern. It seems he can't do anything right. Whether he says something or if he doesn't say something, snide comments are made by the family and no-one comes to his rescue.

Why might this be happening? What is it about Brother Jimmy that makes the family respond to him with snide remarks? Sometimes he actually seems to be two steps ahead of the family which is another problem, and he's in trouble for that as well. For example, we see in this scene how Brother Jimmy is steps ahead of Dad and is already carrying the ladder to help Miss Annie down from the second story window - this being the most obvious solution to get Miss Annie rescued from her room and for that he's scolded- *"Take that ladder back"*.

Jimmy is busy collecting evidence about his position in the family. He can't win, almost as if to say, *'If I say something I'm in trouble and if I don't say something I'm in trouble.'* Where does he fit? With so much time being directed toward Helen and her handicaps, who would even recognize a family member being neglected? By the way, you may notice that Jimmy responds with a few snide remarks himself throughout the story! There's that mirror again!

Neglecting other members of a family, a group member or a team player, happens all the time due to the presence of the handicapped member. 'Handicapped' individuals in this text refer to physical handicaps as well as emotional, mental, social and Spiritual handicaps. A handicapped member can possess a variety of symptoms, not just the deaf and blind. The array of handicapped conditions any family member or team experiences vary to the degree that no two snowflakes are alike, unique to the individual situation. This is not meant to minimize anyone's condition, but certainly Helen does have the cards stacked against her. Parents today could certainly find ways to deal with their 'handicapped' child, since evidence shows that even a child like Helen can be taught, but the parents would have to want to. You would have to want to persevere for the good of the child, no matter the challenge.

Even in a classroom setting a teacher has to deal with the misbehaving (handicapped) children before she can even begin to teach the lesson. *'Stop that, don't do this, and don't touch that, Johnny pay attention!'* In the mean time the 'good' students' sit and wait for the chaos to stop. The good students' freedoms have been robbed by the 'handicapped' student. Teachers know, before long, the good student will also become the unruly (handicapped) student because it doesn't take them long to realize; *'Wow, look at all the attention you can get if you are handicapped. Since the misbehaving (handicapped) student gets attention, I want that, I want attention; maybe I could actually like inappropriate attention. I guess I can only get attention when I am misbehaving. I can get rewarded for my bad behavior.'*

Many children are in the news creating chaos in the community every day. Whoever was arrested certainly had a mother and a father or guardian somewhere. Did those adults give up and neglect their parental responsibility? Telling the world, *'I did the best I could,'* is a cop out. The correct response to a reporter who wants to know more about the son or daughter arrested is; *'I didn't want to know'*. This is called Parent Neglect. To close your eyes and not want to look, not want to know or deal with the family issue; this is totally irresponsible behavior and neglectful to both their own family and the community. To be sure, there are many ample resources available in this day and age for you to seek out the help that may be required for your family, for your neighborhood, for the town, the community and the World. Imagine the incredible negative ripple effect in the community because these ignored and misbehaving children are running around creating chaos and bedlam wherever they go? And all this because parents didn't take on the responsibility and make the effort required as parents. We can idly accept negative ripple effects or we can choose positive ripple effects.

Now imagine the incredible positive ripple effect within the community because the child was taught behaviors meant to benefit themselves, their families and the community. Take one step further and notice the ripple effect for yourself personally. You will sleep better, eat better, feel better, and look better - all of which will help you to be better. By acting better physically and emotionally you now have the time to re-evaluate what you want to accomplish towards reaching your own passion. You won't be tied up in chaos which keeps you far too busy to consider your passions, and what your own gifts to the Universe are. It may mean coming out of hiding and taking an honest inventory of yourself in order to quit denying the Spiritual aches and nudges that says, *'You are not listening'*. Ask yourself; *'If you could do anything you wanted, what would it be?'* What have you longed to do and not done due to giving up your personal life for family 3DL chaos? What actions need to be taken at home so you can have your life back and begin to lead the life the Universe has reserved for you?

The Universe doesn't have its hand in your 3DL; the Universe isn't encouraging more human drama. The Universe has its hand in whatever it takes to awaken you to your potential 4DL. Like Miss Annie is to Helen, the Universe acts as your Miracle Worker. Miss Annie doesn't have her hand in Helen's 3DL, in more human drama. Miss Annie has her hand in whatever it takes to awaken Helen's 4DL.

Possible Miracle Worker Dialog: Context Sensitive

Setting the scene: A Daughter is visiting her Mother. It's the morning of a new day and Mom is reading the morning edition of the paper.

Mom: 'That's it, that's all they are going to do?'
Daughter: 'What are you reading?'
Mom: 'The final court decision was finally handed down having to do with one of the sensational stories of a young mom who killed her children.'
Daughter: Considers for a moment. She thinks, 'Ohhhh, yep, that would be my Mom and her belief about an eye for an eye and a tooth for a tooth. I learned that too.'
Mom: 'Can you believe it, they aren't going to string her up; they aren't even going to put her in the electric chair!'

Daughter: Exhales, thinking – 'How can I handle this in a way that could flip the belief system (BS) as it is? How can I apply the art of communication to affect change?'

Daughter: 'You know what I love about you Mom?... I love that I can count on you to be my Mom!' (This being said with a smile, rather than a hand on the hip!)

Mom: 'What, What?'

Daughter: 'You know I used to think like that. I don't think like that anymore.'

Mom: 'What, What?'

Daughter: 'Do you know anything about this Mommy who killed her children? Have you read or do you know anything about her background?'

Mom: 'No.'

Daughter: 'The article I read a couple of days ago described her life as one of a promiscuous nature. She apparently had sex with her father, step-brother and father-in-law... I forget exactly but the gist is she was sexually abused to the point where she believed sex meant love. I'm not saying that killing her children is ok -ever. The point is she understood on some level that her lifestyle wasn't right and her behavior was trying to express to others that something is seriously wrong. It is as if she were saying, 'Does anyone see me, does anyone care about me'??? She needs help.'

Mom: Sitting quietly, digesting the shift in thought - the paradigm.

Shortly thereafter, everyone is off to create their day, only to come home in the evening with a follow up to the morning's conversation.

Mom: 'You know... all the ladies at today's luncheon were talking about the newspaper article.'

Daughter: 'Oh, I bet.'

Mom: 'I told them what you said.'

Daughter: Thinking—'Wow, how cool, a ripple effect of a different way of thinking influencing a bunch of ladies during a luncheon.'

Mom: 'You know what they said? They said you were crazy!'

Daughter: In a wow stupor of disbelief but not wanting to get wrapped up in the 3DL drama, she took the lightening-flash thoughts racing through her mind to consider what she wanted the end result to be. She decided to stick to the original intention - the art of communication, and not engage in any 3DL responses... 'You know...I get that a lot.' Said with a smile, not a hand on the hip!

3DL or 4DL? What message did the Mom leave with? Notice the pecking order. What role did Mom have, what role does the daughter have? The daughter clearly had her hand in whatever it takes to awaken her Mom to a 4DL.

—⁓⦁⌾⌾⦁⌾⁓—

Put the following in order: Label 1 through 4 in importance according to your beliefs:

___ Children
___ Spouse
___ Work
___ Me

For today... or for the rest of your life if you want - let's change the order to:

1) Me, 2) Spouse, 3) Children, 4) Work

Learn to recognize the person in your family who is left out and overlooked. Help them to realize that you understand what they are going through, and validate their position. With enough evidence collected, before long the 'good' child won't even try to be part of the family. The 'Helen' in your family hogs the limelight; there is no room for anyone else. This member who is overlooked could even be the spouse. Statistics for divorce are prevalent among families who haven't taken the time to realize their own family dynamics especially if the spouse is constantly overlooked for the sake of the handicapped child. This formula for disaster will most certainly unfold if the child comes first over the spouse. The spouse always comes first in a healthy 4DL family dynamic; this encourages the support you both need from each other. Work with each other, plan together, and talk everything over with each other.

What else can cause a 3DL family situation? Take a moment to notice the amount of exhaustion experienced due to the overwhelming 3DL chaos in the home. Notice this constant negative energy that causes a variety of emotional responses: depression, anxiety, helplessness, hopelessness, giving up attitude, withdrawal, hiding out, escape, denial… none of which are solutions. Commit to making a difference in your home, commit to finding a solution or at least find an expert to teach new tools. You owe it to yourself and to your family. You are the adult and you are the parent. It is time for those of us with children to become responsible and take on an adult grownup role. It is our job and there is no greater job than to love a child enough to do right by them.

Don't give up or give in just because you didn't want to 'hear' the noise, the tantrum, the whining, and the complaining from your child. What is the ultimate cost to the family? What family freedoms would you be relinquishing if the child always had their own way? Were they allowed to be unruly and create chaos in the home? Don't give up- try, try and try again. It is through this insistent effort - the insistent and redirecting management of an unruly child that will enable other family members to secure their rightful place in the home.

Recognize that you won't be able to make a significant difference until you are in touch with your Spirit and what *you* really want, which means you have to put yourself first. This probably feels a lot like being selfish. You may have been taught that putting yourself first is selfish behavior. Be aware that there is a balance between how far the pendulum can swing from one side to the other - either swinging toward 'too selfish' or 'not selfish' enough. Finding the just right balance is difficult but none the less this leads to creating a better balance.

When you keep others as your priority, then you are in *their* human drama. Chances are you are too available to fix the latest dilemma and most likely are enabling as a result. If you are in their human drama and in their humanism, it would be impossible for you to be in *your* Spirit. This is a key point to recognize. If you cannot stay out of their business, then you really don't want to know about *your* Spirit's wants and needs. Being there for everyone but yourself is about being afraid to look at the power of your own potential. You prefer to stay busy addressing everyone else's wants and needs. *'What an unselfish person you are!'* This looks like you are not being the least bit selfish - how gallant. Today I am suggesting that you keep yourself first which has nothing to do with being selfish and everything to do with taking care of yourself. Taking care of you is a choice and has nothing to do with being selfish. The priority is to take care of YOU? Give yourself this permission.

Notice the gauge of how far the pendulum now swings. If you can't detach yourself with an appropriate more balanced pendulum swing, it may be a good idea to look at the overpowering 'need to be needed' dis-ease. The dreaded 'need to be needed' is a great example of human drama taking over, especially for women. We have been taught since we were little girls to be the caretakers and nurturers to those around us. We have learned this very well. On top of that, many of us were taught it wasn't nice to put ourselves first until we take care of everyone else. What we have learned is that our value depends on how much we are needed and how much we give of ourselves and do for others. Worse is the belief of placing more value on how others see us rather than on how we see ourselves.

Consider that you are not allowing yourself to follow the Universes' plan when you aren't on the front burner. You are following another's plan and making that more important than what you *should* be doing. 'Doing' for others does not allow you to hear the unique plan Divinely orchestrated just for you. You are too busy and most likely not able to even recognize the Universe's effort to get a hold of you.

'Me!? Put me first?' What a thought! How foreign, how uncomfortable this may feel. Putting yourself first requires having an intimate relationship with yourself. Know yourself inside and out enough to like yourself, to love yourself. Allow yourself to take the time to understand your most intimate thoughts and emotions. Allow yourself to do what might feel 'over the top' selfish to some. Be selfish enough to grow and develop, to be the most incredible person you are here to be. Ask yourself pointed questions about what would give you the most joy in life. What is the intent of all this? Simply put, to understand your

Spiritual wants and needs, you have to put yourself on the front burner of life. There is a balance to be achieved here. You can balance family, friends and spouse while keeping yourself on the front burner. Practice. Find the joy while practicing being intimate with yourself, and discover your Spirit.

What a Miracle Worker Would Share

There are two important points in this scene. 1) The symbolism of Helen locking out the one individual in her life that could make the difference in her world. 2) Recognize the amount of effort, time and energy needed for the handicapped child in your family over the detriment of the healthier members of the family.

It is our duty and should be our joy, parent or not, to bring into this world and leave within this world, circumstances and opportunities which will better this world. Remember being taught by your parents, *'Leave the place better than you found it!'* There is a lot of talk about 'green' these days. From recycling to a raised awareness about landfills, bringing and reusing canvas bags instead of plastic bags for groceries. Cleaning and picking up on highways, in parks… leaving the world better off; leave the world in a better state than in which we found it. What will the benefit be for the future, for the grandchildren?

How do we use this same amount of effort and clean up our children? How do we make our children the priority and make them 'green'? Maybe the real question to ask is, is inner discipline necessary to redirect the child's behavior? Will you work at it, will you try? Many times you will hear excuses about parents today. Phrases like *'They did the best they could!'* This statement is nothing more than a cop out. There is always another idea, suggestion, and opportunity available to learn a new way, a new tool, even in consulting a new expert. It may be out of your comfort zone and certainly something to be worked at. After all, your children are your responsibility. You owe it to the community at large. If your child exhibits socially disturbing behaviors how do you in good conscience allow them out into your neighborhood and community to hurt and vandalize others? How will a child who has not been diligently looked after and taught manners, or who has never been taught the difference between right from wrong, truly act in the community? Certainly the identical negative behaviors a child exhibits inside the home are sure to be mimicked outside the home. Don't be fooled, since these actions reflect the only behavior the child knows.

Share your gifts, your purpose with the world. We all have much to do, and being 'busy' with others is not part of the plan. Do not rob the Universe of the gift that you are. Consciously connect this month to how you stay busy with others so you don't have to listen to the plan, so you don't have to act on the plan. Where should you focus your intention? Consider the valuable talent, tools and gifts you could offer the world. Honor the gift you are and have a little me, me, me time! The Angels are dancing and singing… *"Ahhhh"*.

3DL or 4DL is a choice, which lifestyle do you choose?

Intention– *Synonyms*–deliberate, intended, willed, done on purpose, planned, purposeful, designed, premeditated, contemplated, voluntary, calculated

OR

Intention– *Antonyms*–accidental, fortuitous, inadvertent, unintentional, unplanned.

Scene Ten

Empower the Ones You Love

Captain Keller yells to Jimmy to bring back the ladder.

Captain Keller: *Jimmy! Bring me a ladder!*
Captain Keller: *Miss Sullivan!*
Miss Annie: *Yes, Captain Keller?*
Captain Keller: *Come out of your window onto the roof.*
Miss Annie: *Oh, you have a ladder. How thoughtful.*
Captain Keller: *Come down, Miss Sullivan.*
Miss Annie: *I don't see how I can.*
Captain Keller: *I intend to carry you.*
Miss Annie: *Oh, no. It's very chivalrous of you, but I'd really prefer to...*
Captain Keller: *Miss Sullivan, follow instructions. I will not have you also tumblin' out of our windows. I hope this is not a sample of what we may expect from you. In the way of simplifyin' the work of looking after Helen.*
Miss Annie: *Captain Keller, I'm perfectly able to go down a ladder under my own steam.*
Captain Keller: *I doubt it, Miss Sullivan. Simply hold onto my neck. My neck, Miss Sullivan!*
Miss Annie: *I'm sorry to inconvenience you this way--*
Captain Keller: *No inconvenience other than taking that door down and replacing the lock if we can't find the key.*
Miss Annie: *I'll look everywhere for it.*

In this scene it seems Captain Keller is very gentlemanly, very gallant in his rescue of Miss Annie from the roof top. Miss Annie even calls Captain Keller chivalrous. You would expect nothing less from a true Southern gentleman.

64

There is a time to help one another and then there are the times when helping turns into over-helping, which is called enabling. I'm sure this can be a difficult distinction for any man, especially a southern gentleman, a Captain in the army. Enabling is something every parent needs to be acutely aware of. We can do and overdo, we can help and over-help and not even realize we are getting these actions confused with what is the correct definition of help. More importantly, notice how over-helping a child can rob the individual of having to dig deep within to reach for their Spirit and find answers and solutions for themselves. In this particular scene when Miss Annie suggests she can get down the ladder on her own, Captain Keller does not honor this request. How many times does a child know how to handle a new task by themselves and we don't honor their request. We just do it for them anyway, after all-- *'It's quicker.'*

Helping a child who is a handicapped member of the family is especially important. Of course the child needs help, but in these cases we need to pause momentarily and consider whether or not helping a child is really more about hindrance. Or maybe helping a child is about making you feel good for being the competent adult who has the answers and solutions. Or maybe you are over compensating for something a parent might feel guilty about. Certainly rescuing anyone helps fill up your own emotional piggy bank, floats your boat, albeit by selfishly filling a personal void. We all want to feel purposeful, needed and valuable. Interesting though, if we look at this a bit closer, what does the child eventually learn? The 'mental gymnastics' misguided belief teaches the child; *'I don't have to do anything in life because someone will do it for me. As long as I milk this wound I can get people to do things for me.'* I don't believe we really want any child to learn this message, but this is often the painful reality.

The next time you are about to do something for a child ask yourself if it is actually necessary to help or can this child do the task for themselves? The next time you are about to do something for an adult ask yourself if it is actually necessary to help or can this individual do the task themselves? Let them know you recognized that this task was something they could do for themselves and if they needed help you are available, and then walk away and leave them with the task.

Later be sure to make a comment about the job well done even if it wasn't done to your total liking, unless you really want to do the job for them! Recognize a task not done well is a form of communicating that the individual wants you to rescue and fix the problem. If they do a poor enough job then the adult won't ask them to do it again, right? Everybody knows this, you know this and a child really knows this; that includes any child, regardless of age!

Keeping all this in mind, did you end up doing the task anyway, or when you walked away after allowing the child to handle the task, did you feel less valuable, not needed or less purposeful? This may be a problem to consider. The next time you are about to do something for an individual and then do it, even though you know the individual could do the task themselves, ask yourself; 'How does staying busy keep me from doing what I need to be doing for myself right now?' What are your joys, passions and dreams and how are you fulfilling them? How are you neglecting your Spirit, how are you dismissing and resisting all inner Spiritual nudges?

To close your eyes and not to want to look, know or deal with your own Spirit is totally irresponsible and neglectful to yourself as an individual as well as the community and the world at large. All of us are capable of balancing our dreams and passions with our family responsibilities especially when there is minimal chaos, drama and dysfunction. Dreams and passions cannot be fulfilled if there is a great deal of chaos and dysfunction in the family, there is just too much distraction. We all have a gift to give to the Universe. We may be afraid to work and encourage our talents; the amount of inner stirring and excitement attached to this gift development is so powerful it can be an overwhelming feeling. All kinds of fears can crop up when pursuing dreams and aspirations. It's so much easier to just stay busy, busy, busy.

Scene Seven is all about Brother Jimmy, included in the scene text is the topic of enablement. This next paragraph is taken from that scene. Enablement has such a powerful crippling effect on anyone, especially a child who has a handicap or pretends a handicap for the purposes of avoiding responsibility and accountability, to be allowed to act helpless. Enablement is so often misunderstood by people that repeating this information on the topic from <u>Scene Seven – Attention Seeking</u> is so important to reinforce, especially if you can recognize yourself as the overstepping helper/enabler. It's what a Miracle Worker would share…

'When is helping overstepping and infringing on the truth of enablement? Helping is no longer helpful when the help doesn't help foster or develop independence. In that case, helping is now enabling. Enablement is when we spend so much time helping we lose focus on the self. Enablement is when we can't take the time to create our own lives because we're too busy creating someone else's life. Enablement is when we are the Spiritual essence of another and not our own Spiritual self; we've given up our own lives, our own Spirit. Enablement looks and feels like a noble thing to do… so giving, so selfless. Don't be fooled, don't deny the truth of your need to be needed, look good, or be purposeful.'

Each day and maybe each moment, ask yourself to recognize what one task you know the adult/child can do for themselves, and then let them do it. Allow the adult/child to risk making mistakes throughout their growing-up years. When you, as the adult, start off early in children's lives to encourage self reliance, the mistakes are minor and easily recoverable because they are little people with little mistakes. Be aware of how learning curves occur best when rescuing the child isn't part of the learning curve. For the older individual, they may fall a little harder but they do have more tools to work with. Instead of fixing, rescuing and enabling, ask pointed questions about how they will help themselves. *'What good ideas do you have? What solutions could you think about?'* Give up the need to be the answer to all their problems, instead reach their Spirit, that internal place and say; *'Wow that's interesting what will you do to handle that?'* Feel the depth of the difference with these questions. Ask all kinds of questions so the child is encouraged to reach deep within themselves for solutions.

———— ⚜ ————

Possible Miracle Worker Dialog: Context Sensitive

Let's take an example of a young girl driving home from college for a weekend visit. It's almost midnight and she just got off of work. The drive is at least two hours long. She calls you up a half hour into the trip and says something is wrong with the car. You encourage her to drive safely and to keep a steady course home. Within minutes she calls to say she's stranded, the car died, and it won't start up again. She was able to veer off onto an exit but she was still in the road unable to coast onto the grass. Ugh!

As a parent, a million thoughts go through your mind, you panic. Words cannot describe how overly concerned you are. It's late, she's on a freeway, it's dark, she's a young girl, there's crazies out there, anything could happen. You know the impossibility of hopping in the car to rescue and fix everything for her, she's an hour and half away. You may think to yourself – *'Where's my broom?'* You can hear panic in her voice. What do you do? Thank goodness there are cell phones and AAA road service.

Consider the following responses rather than screaming, panicking, lecturing, yelling, freaking modes. Start with listening. Let the young adult share with you everything that happened from the minute she got in the car to the minute she sensed something was wrong. Allow her to express everything she wants. Validate all comments by saying and using only the vowels such as 'Ahhh!', 'Ohhh!', and 'Umm!' Let her expound on all the thoughts and ideas that ran through her head as she realized the predicament she would be in if she were to truly break down. Her worst fears are confirmed, she calls you first. You know there isn't much you can do on your end. What is left to do? You could empower her; help her draw out from deep within her, her inner strengths that need to surface and come up with some good ideas and solutions. *'Honey, I'm going to hang up now, pull your thoughts together, and remember you have AAA. Take a minute to think about what to do. I trust your judgments. Call me back when you have a game plan.'*

Of course, every minute seems like an hour. She doesn't call back, you know she's alone, you know there are crazies out at this time of night, and you know the Florida mosquitoes are biting her. Amazing how the imagination can run amok with you. You tell yourself to remain cool. More than enough time has gone by and she hasn't called back, you worry even more about the possible dangers out there so you call her back. The phone rings and rings with no pick up. You hang up distraught, there's nothing you can do but wait. You begin to wrack your brain considering who you know in that area that might be able to help. Anyone? Seconds go by and she's calling back. *'Mom, I have called AAA and they have all the details of where I am. They wanted to know if I wanted the police to come and I said 'Yes,--Ohhh-ohhh!'* all of a sudden she's yelling and screaming almost out of control into the phone.

What now? She's losing her inner strength, you don't have a clue what's going on, and you just know it can't be good. You yell into the phone *'Stop!'* You are prepared to give her the necessary encouragement to pull herself together no matter what the problem. She goes into a whole yelling screaming exclamation about how two cars almost collided and crashed into her because she's in the way, but… they didn't. She regains some composure. You stay on the phone with her until the police arrive, asking if she double checked to know her hazard lights are on and she's locked the doors which she's, of course, already handled. After all… you brought her up in 4DL; she knows how to go within for answers and solutions, because you let her. Even still, you warn her about 'helpful' police and AAA people, although you don't want to alarm her!

Within ten minutes she calls you again and gives you the whole run down how she's safe and how she's figured out the rest of her dilemma. Of course she doesn't come home that night, the car needs repair, she's back in her dorm room, and it's now almost two o'clock. Knowing you both need to get some sleep, you leave her with *'You know what I love about you, I love that you know how to take care of yourself.'* That being the most important message you want her to walk away with. All of her good ideas might not have been your good ideas, but they were hers and she's safe and sound in her own dorm in her own bed. Dear Angels- *"Ahhhh!"*

—∿∿⟨⟩∿∿—

What a Miracle Worker Would Share

No matter the problem or dilemma and rest assured there *will* be problems and dilemmas, how can we get into the mode of a 4DL empowering response instead of the all-to-common 3DL human reactive freak out over reactions?

When at all possible, start regarding the child as an equal, even the little one year old. This can certainly be a bit difficult to do since you held them as infants - so helpless for all their needs in life. But they do grow and they do grow up. Let loose the apron strings, give up some control, and allow them their mistakes. Be close by to pick them up when they truly hurt themselves otherwise let them pick themselves up. Basically, get out of the way. Be available to ask pointed questions, coming from a place of curiosity rather than as a competent giant of a parent, bulleting them with criticisms and pointing out what is wrong rather than what is right in their world. Tell them how clever they are, what a great idea that was, ask them to teach you about the latest new fangled gimmick. Of course the message you really want them to be left with is that they themselves are clever in their own right, they do have good ideas, and they are knowledgeable and capable in anything they do. Why? One day they may be in a situation where they will need to be clever with their own good ideas, and be knowledgeable enough to take care of themselves. This is Divinely orchestrated, and its only a matter of time for a specific challenge/opportunity to present itself - it is an expected piece to the game of life.

Practice and rehearse these new solutions for yourself. Start to adjust your vocabulary with new thought patterns, with these new solutions. Recognize the spoken statements that are empowering and 4DL based. Put them in your back pocket and be prepared to pull them out at the appropriate times. Know that the Universe will present you with opportunities to practice. More importantly, you will begin to notice how the Universe will present opportunity after opportunity until your responses become more of a 4DL healthy response. 3DL responses are just an invitation begging for the Universe to jump in with an intervention to provide another opportunity, because these 3DL types of responses are not healthy and represent a lesson still to be overcome. Choose 4DL and be amazed at the results - the independent, capable, responsible and accountable adult/children you have brought into this world. The Angels sing knowing you are growing up too! *"Ahhhh"!*

Be proud of yourself for constantly reaching your inner discipline. Know your health and wealth depends upon your doing right, especially when it comes to children. Know that you cannot fool your heart. When you don't take the necessary steps, know you are breaking your heart and your health will reflect the inconsistencies. You will begin to notice your body's dis-ease. You will be as ill and as sick as your secrets, especially the secrets where your mind strives and continues to try to fool your heart. By Universal Law you are accountable and you will indeed experience the consequences. Some call that Karma.

3DL or 4DL is a choice, which lifestyle do you choose?

Empower– *Synonyms*–authorize, sanction, invest, license, permit, allow, enable, commission, delegate.

OR

Empower– *Antonyms*–restrain, disbar, divest of power, disallow, forbid, enjoin.

Scene Eleven

Adaptable Moments

Once Miss Annie is down from the roof she confirms her belief that Helen is quite clever, cunning and very intelligent. Lucky for Helen, or perhaps not, Miss Annie tells her she doesn't have anything else to do or anywhere else to go but to work with Helen!

Miss Annie: You devil. Oh, you think I'm so easily gotten rid of? You've got a thing or two to learn first. I've got nothing else to do, and nowhere to go.
Captain: Miss Sullivan!

In this scene, Miss Annie is in her room and Helen just spilled the ink all over the desk Miss Annie is sitting at working on her journal.

Miss Annie: (Miss Annie writes a letter) …and nobody here has attempted to control her. The greatest problem I have is how to discipline her without breaking her spirit. (gasp, Helen has just spilt the ink) Ink. Ink. It has a name. Down, under, up. And be careful of the needle. (Helen is playing with a sewing card) Right. You keep out of the ink and perhaps I can keep out of --the soup. (gasp, Helen sticks herself) All right, all right. Let's try temperance. Bad… girl. Good… girl. Yes. Very good girl.

Miss Annie takes advantage of every teachable moment available to her. She takes every opportunity that comes her way as another opportunity to get Helen to 'see'. Miss Annie can't use the typical external means of seeing or hearing to help Helen connect to the world, so she needs to reach her from her Spirit… from within her.

Remember that time in first grade or maybe kindergarten when you read your very first word? You sat in your little school desk and pulled

72

all the sounds together slowly, realizing if you said them quick and fast the letters said a word you were familiar with. Remember how you felt? Were you proud of yourself? Did the Angels sing at that moment? It was that very *eureka!* moment when you reached within and figured out there was a whole new world to explore, and then your world opened up. Thinking back, you may not remember the actual goose bumps or the chills running down your neck, but what you definitely experienced was a 4DL feeling, a true moment of celebration. You couldn't wait to read to anyone who would listen! You wanted to read all day every day, just to have the exhilaration of putting the words together. Of course, none of that could have happened if you were an unruly student, cutting up and creating drama in the classroom. You would have been left just as handicapped as Helen-- deaf and blind to reading. You wouldn't be able to gain enough self control to even sit long enough to hear the instructions from the teacher to learn how to read. You wouldn't be able to see or hear what the teacher was saying to you; you would be drowning in noisy drama!

Hollywood, California knows all about 4DL feelings. The directors and creators of movies weave their stories with the purpose of 'moving' you, moving your Spirit. They want you to walk away all tingly and excited about the heartfelt movie you just watched so you'll want to see it again and again. But what did you walk away with? Did you simply enjoy the storyline where the bad guy was finally caught and the good guy was triumphant? You knew who the bad guy was; they were always in black and the good guys were always in white. They even rode a black horse and a white horse. Or what about the storyline where the guy finally wins over the girl? These stories all seem to go something like: boy meets girl, boy loses girl, and then boy wins girl's heart.

We all enjoy these movies, although sometimes they are a little bit too 'girly' (a chick flick) for the guys to want to watch with us ladies. Next time you are watching one of these heartfelt 4DL movies, watch while keeping the director and producer in mind. What camera effects did they use to make their points? What was the music like? Did you hear the music; have you ever noticed how the Orchestra crescendos right at the exact moment where you actually feel goose bumps and chills down your neck? How deliberate, how purposeful; all great examples of 4DL! Could it be this same type of feeling we search and long for? This 4DL feeling is what we want more of, which is why we pay the movie prices? Is this the reason we have to be at the very first showing of the new movie being advertised? Is this one of the reasons we enjoy going to plays and operas? Is this the reason we go to concerts? It rocks our Soul, it touches our Spirit, and it moves us, its 4DL. Even the Helen Keller story reaches us in very much the same way. During the breakfast scene struggle we felt it, and especially by the water pump when Helen first connects to what words are, just like you did when you read your first word. Tingly all over; *"Ahhhh"* moments for sure.

Without the ability to use words, Miss Annie doesn't give up, she tries and tries again. She understands Helen's world will open up the moment she understands the meaning of words, but how in this world do you get her to sit still long enough so that she can grasp the difference?

Take this as an example for yourself not to give up on your 'handicapped' child. Take every opportunity presented to you as an adaptable moment, a teachable moment. What new idea will you try today, what new strategy? Are you stuck? Can't think of what to do? Is anger or maybe pity for the child so strong and powerful within you that you can't even think, let alone think of a new idea? Try doing the opposite. Try the exact opposite of the strategy you are currently using.

For example, if you traditionally yell at your child to get them to submit, try extending your arms out as if you were asking for a hug. The child may be stunned by this gesture, but keep your arms out until he gets the idea that you are nonverbally asking for a hug. When he comes forward, grab him up in a bear hug squeezing with his legs dangling from the ground. Don't let him go. Hold him long enough so that you can feel the anger leave both of your beings. Notice the change between you and your child. When you see love and understanding in the mirror, you will receive love and understanding. (If he fights harder he didn't feel the love!)

Possible Miracle Worker Dialog: Context Sensitive

Notice how you can win cooperation with love. Play the hugging game. Extend your arms to hug your child and don't let go - tell them; *'I love you so much. I'm never going to let you go. No, no (as they try to escape), don't leave, don't leave!'* Loosen the hug lightly as they begin to slide off your lap. This is especially effective for the child who seeks inappropriate attention. Play with them and tell them you never want them to go, pouting while he continues to try and escape your grasp. Notice the results, the child won't need your attention as much because this kind of love and attention makes the child re-evaluate his belief that you don't spend enough time with him or maybe he already has decided you really don't love him.

Repeat the hugging game as often as possible, especially if the relationship is disturbed and the child shows signs of being lonely, sad, or defeated. You may not understand how they could possibly feel this way, but they very well may, in their little minds. It really doesn't matter the reason why, as long as we know. Once we recognize their feelings we will know how to flip that belief system; our job as parents is to flip that BS! Fill up their emotional piggy bank. Notice afterwards how the child begins to play alone happily, he learns self sufficiency, and he learns autonomy. His emotional piggy bank is full and now he can move along in his work, his job - to play. Through play the children will learn how to give total focus, learning to be deeply involved in their task, the same energy they will need as adults focusing on adult tasks.

What a Miracle Worker Would Share

Amazingly, sometimes we get in a rut of repeating the same strategy over and over in life, even with our children. It is very helpful to discover why the response is the same. Stop and process why the response is not more creative, ingenious or even fun. Ask where the anger is really coming from. Are you too tired to be creative, a sure sign of depression and being overwhelmed? How could you be more adaptable?

Take a minute and remember your child's early years. There they are crawling around the floor of your home. They touch everything they can reach. They love all kinds of buttons, buttons on the remote, the buttons on the television, they love the buttons on the phone, and they love the buttons on the computer. If there is a button, they will find it and push it. They will find *your* buttons and push them too! The child may have pushed your buttons to the point of anger. Anger is the key; this is where to look when you take some time to process what really happened. Take that necessary time. What I can tell you is-- you are never truly angry at the individual standing in front of you. You are never angry at the child. You are angry about how they made you feel because you didn't get the desired result you wanted. Being angry when *'They never listen!'* brings up all kinds of emotional reasons like:

'They never listen!' - really means…
- I'm not loved.
- I feel rejected.
- They don't care.
- I don't feel valuable.
- They don't respect me.
- I'm not an effective parent.
- They don't respect me as a parent.

These are all very personal reasons why you may be angry and frustrated. Maybe you really needed the hug more than your child. To close your eyes and not to want to look, know or deal with this or any similar family issue is truthfully irresponsible and neglectful to yourself, your own family as well as the community and by extension, the world. Encourage yourself to find new solutions; be the clever self that you are and yes; it's okay to ask for hugs. That's why we are here, to experience everything human as the Spiritual beings we are and something truly vital like hugs are at the top of the list of human experiences. I think I hear a choir of Angels… *"Ahhhh!"*

3DL or 4DL is a choice, which lifestyle do you choose?

Adaptable– *Synonyms–*flexible, compliant, open-minded, easygoing, accommodating, malleable, amenable

OR

Adaptable– *Antonyms–*uptight, inflexible, nonadjustable, unalterable, fixed, closed-minded

Scene Twelve

Accepting Life's Adversities

In this scene Mom comes into Miss Annie's room and notices a strange game being played...

Kate: What are you saying to her?

Miss Annie: Oh, I was just making conversation. Saying it was a sewing card.

Kate: Does that mean that to her?

Miss Annie: Oh, no. She won't know what spelling is till she knows what a word is.

Kate: The Cap'n says it's like spellin' to a fence post.

Miss Annie: Does he, now?

Kate: Is it?

Miss Annie: No. It's how I watch you talk to the baby.

Kate: The baby?

Miss Annie: Any baby. It's gibberish. Grown-up gibberish. Baby-talk gibberish. Do they understand one word of it to start? Somehow they begin to. If they hear it; I'm letting Helen hear it.

Kate: Other children are not... impaired.

Miss Annie: Oh, there's nothing impaired in that head. It works like a mousetrap!

Kate: And... when will she learn?

Miss Annie: Maybe after a million words. Perhaps you'd like to read Dr Howe on the question of words.

Kate: I should like also to learn those... letters, Miss Annie.

Miss Annie: I'll teach them to you tomorrow morning. That makes only half a million each!

The above scene represents heartfelt paradigm shifts. How can we discover the gift of personal adversity and transform suffering and confusion into growth for a more meaningful life? Kate has her Mommy hat on, and this Mom needs some reassurance. How simple Miss Annie makes working with Helen. Miss Annie compares Helen's learning equal to a baby's learning. Miss Annie explains to Mom on a level Mom can understand since she has an infant in the house to compare. What a great paradigm Miss Annie comes up with to shift Kate in a way that makes so much sense. Miss Annie gives Mom the desperate hope she has so longed for. It's all back to basics, very simple basics. Miss Annie starts with one word items like: d.o.l.l., c.a.k.e. or w.a.t.e.r. Like a puppy you 'housebreak,' one word commands are used like 'sit, come, or stay'. Whatever the adversity is going on in your home, look for the simplicity in the situation, and simplify your responses. One-word responses are a great way to simplify; this leaves little room for miscommunication.

We often feel overwhelmed with new life challenges/opportunities and the answer was right in front of us. Many times the answer ended up being an easier solution then we could have ever have imagined. Less is more. Consider how much talking, arguing, scolding and lecturing when one word sentences could work or even an extension of our arms, a nonverbal expression of a need for a hug to diffuse the moment. There are so many options available, so many different ways to improvise. Decide to rummage around in your tool box, dig for a few of those rusty tools and discern for yourself which tool you might want to shine up and use for that... special moment.

Understandably, Helen's handicap could make any parent feel overwhelmed. The difference in the Keller family overall was they were ready and willing to finally work it. Like a motto 'Work it!' 'Work it!' 'Work it!' Not quite a one word command but I think you get it; you may have to learn a new tool, a new skill. This may make you initially uncomfortable and take you out of your comfort box. Go there anyway; these challenges/opportunities are before you for a reason. Don't go into avoidance. Like the Keller family, maybe your family situation will be the example needed for other families to admire enough to want to learn from. We may not know the reasons why nor do we always understand the Divine plan but that doesn't mean we couldn't put our best foot forward and make better choices for the best outcome possible for your child, with a bonus of a ripple effect for those around you. Before you abandon your charge; 'Work it!' 'Work it!' 'Work it'! You owe this to yourself and you owe this to your child. Find the gift in your personal adversity.

Mom is still not sure, under the circumstances; *"Other children are not... impaired"*. Miss Annie doesn't buy into that type of thinking. She doesn't agree with it, why would she, where would it get her? At this stage of the story it's too early to feel like there is no hope. The Keller's family dilemma is a clear example of how the change agent will do well to respond in a positive encouraging way. The Keller's need hope and believe their cup is half full of hope rather than believing it is half empty with hardly any hope.

Miss Annie's experience as a blind child understands the value of 'words'. Miss Annie experienced this herself while growing up and even begged to go to school. Someone with Miss Annie's experience would know exactly what to do with a child with Helen's handicaps. Miss Annie was Helen. There could be no better teacher for the Kellers. Somewhere along the line of growing up in an institution, Miss Annie learned about this place called school. Miss Annie discovered and understood that learning reading, writing and arithmetic would make the difference in her life.

(Woman#1) They're all here. (Woman #2) Talk to them. (Woman #3) You can get out. Talk to them. All the investigators are here. That's Mr. Sanborn. He's the commissioner. Talk to him. You might get out. Miss Annie: Mr. Sanborn? Mr. Sanborn, I want to go to school.

If Miss Annie were ever to be in a downward depressive emotional spiral moment – and who wouldn't when you understand Miss Annie's unfortunate childhood years – she doesn't allow herself to stay down long. A challenge/opportunity has presented itself and this is the moment to jump on it! You could imagine little Annie crying out to the Universe *"Why me Lord? Why is this happening to me: How come I can't have the life like other children in a secure home with healthy parents, why me?"* We all have those moments, we should have those moments. Moments like these propel us to the next moment of opportunity. When we become sick and tired of being sick and tired we are ready to accept and seek out change. Little Annie was ready...for school.

———————

Possible Miracle Worker's Dialog- Context Sensitive

From time to time you may need to have a dialog with yourself, maybe every day. Each day could provide opportunities/challenges that are full of confusion and angst. Exhale and give yourself a pep talk while you sit patiently waiting for life to play out. Give yourself a little smile indicating having trust and faith the Universe is busy creating the next best situation. Patiently let it come to you. All we have to do is be available to recognize it!

Others may need a reminder... *'You are in the middle of overcoming your life's lesson. This is your personal adversity! You are having a Spiritual Experience; you are a very strong Soul.'*

———————

Anne Sullivan Macy (1866 - 1936)

"Anne was born on April 14, 1866 in Feeding Hills, Massachusetts. Though she was called Anne or Annie from the very beginning, her baptismal certificate identifies her as Johanna Mansfield Sullivan. Her parents, Thomas Sullivan and Alice Cloesy Sullivan, were poor, illiterate Irish immigrants. Her mother was frail, suffering from tuberculosis. Her father was unskilled and alcoholic.

Little or nothing in her early years encouraged or supported her lively, inquiring mind. She was unschooled; hot tempered; nearly blind from untreated trachoma by age seven; and, on her mother's death when Anne was eight years old, left to deal with her abusive father and maintain their dilapidated home. Two years later Thomas Sullivan abandoned his family.

On February 22, 1876, Anne and her brother Jimmie were sent to the state almshouse in Tewksbury, Massachusetts. Jimmie, who was younger than Anne and had been born with a tubercular hip, died a short time later. Anne spent four years at Tewksbury, enduring the grief of her brother's death and the disappointment of two unsuccessful eye operations. Then, as a result of her direct plea to a state official who had come to inspect the Tewksbury almshouse, she was allowed to leave and enroll in the Perkins School for the Blind in Boston, Massachusetts. Her life changed profoundly at that point.

At Perkins, in October 1880, Anne finally began her academic education - quickly learning to read and write. She also learned to use the manual alphabet in order to communicate with a friend who was deaf as well as blind. That particular skill opened the door to her future and a life of remarkable achievements. While at Perkins, Anne had several successful eye operations, which improved her sight significantly. In 1886 she graduated from Perkins as valedictorian of her class. A short time later, Anne accepted the Keller family's offer to come to Tuscumbia, Alabama, to tutor their blind, deaf, mute daughter, Helen.

In March of 1887 Anne began her lifelong role as Helen Keller's beloved Teacher. In short order she managed to make contact with the angry, rebellious child, who learned eagerly and quickly once Anne had gained her confidence. Anne was Helen's educator for thirteen years and, in 1900, accompanied her to Cambridge, Massachusetts, where Helen was admitted to Radcliffe College. Anne went with Helen to every class, spelling into her hand all the lectures, demonstrations, and assignments. When Helen received her bachelor of arts degree, it was a triumph for both women. While Anne was not officially a student, she had gained a college education."
AFB, American Foundation for the Blind

Spiritually we know there are no coincidences. Everything happens for a reason, everything is in Divine order. We may not always understand, we may *never* understand. In Miss Annie's case, her life experience was specifically and Divinely designed to be a ripple effect to help Helen and the Keller family. Helen's life story was specifically and Divinely designed to have a ripple effect to help the world. My life was specifically and Divinely designed to have a ripple effect to re-ignite *The Miracle Worker* story. What is your family's Divine design?

What a Miracle Worker Would Share

Do not become overwhelmed with your personal life story, look for the simplicity in the situation, and know that nothing is impossible. What feels impossible, boring, tiresome, grueling indicates an actual step ready to be taken. Sometimes being tired of the negative attitude or emotion will prompt an action. Even if you take small steps, take the small step. Take any step. Prevent the dis-ease you currently feel and take an action. Stay upbeat and positive. This is a choice. To stay encouraged rather than discouraged is a choice in attitude. Be the example in your home, be courageous, be the hero that lifts everyone up. Solicit the help of family and friends, win cooperation, be the cheerleader. Courageously take on the challenge/opportunity.

Remember, don't get all hung up in the 'whys' of life. *'Why me, why my family, why, why, why?'* The word 'why' is *whiney,* like a two year old having a temper tantrum. To be whiney, feeling like a victim and having tantrums is a choice. Shift to the gift of your life, shift to believing and accept you have been chosen, you are the one designed to handle your challenges/opportunities in a Divinely perfected way. Pick yourself up; dust yourself off, give up playing the victim. Reach way down, deep to your core, to the essence of which you are, your Spirit and ask firmly *'What?'* Using the word *'What?'* is a strong and powerful question! Pose this very simple one word question and be amazed at the answer you hear. Listen and accept the next very good idea that comes to your mind.

Enough already! Get out there! Be strong, and 'Work It.' The Angels are with you, listen…*"Ahhhh!"*

3DL or 4DL is a choice, which lifestyle do you choose?

Accept– *Synonyms*–agree to, go along, assent to, receive willingly, and receive with favor

OR

Accept– *Antonyms*–refuse, reject, decline, spurn, turn down, resist, disown, deny, disavow

Scene Thirteen

Choose Being Lucky

In this scene, Kate is ready for Helen to go to bed. Helen stabs Miss Annie with a sewing needle and Kate gives Helen some cake!

Kate: *It's her bedtime.*
Miss Annie: *Yes. Ow! (Helen, sticks Miss Annie with the needle)*
Kate: *I'm sorry Miss Annie*
Miss Annie: *Why does she get a reward for stabbing me? (Mom gives Helen some cake.)*
Kate: *There are so many times she simply cannot be compelled.*
Miss Annie: *Yes. I'm the same way myself.*
Kate: *Goodnight.*

In this scene, Kate rewards Helen for inappropriate behavior. It seems Mom's apron is full of treats for Helen, used as a tool to reward, motivate, or to get Helen's attention. This is a huge clue Miss Annie observes. Rewarding bad behavior is a notion that has to be undone in the Keller family. Miss Annie discovers through her observations many monumental obstacles to overcome within the first 24 hours of her visit. Miss Annie certainly has her work cut out for her.

There are many misguided beliefs about rewards and punishments that adults embrace. The biggest misconception is to believe and expect there will be an honest behavior change due to the reward or the punishment. Unfortunately any reward or punishment is really just an external control, a band aid fix, the quick fix, the easier remedy. Typically employed for the moment by the adult in the situation, rewards and punishment are used to get everything and everyone under instant control. Rewards and punishment don't meet the child on an internal level; this method doesn't lend itself as a successful and positive internal motivator only a negative external control. Results (if any) will only show themselves as external conducers. The child doesn't learn to do things because they want to and it's the right thing to do, the child learns to do things because he wants the carrot, the toy, the tangible item. The child doesn't learn about the good energetic 4DL feeling. What the child learns is how many 'toys' he/she can collect, which is more in line with 3DL thinking. Which mode of thinking do you want your child to learn? Which mode of thinking will ultimately make a child feel genuinely happy?

Looking at rewards as an example, the child isn't reached and encouraged from that special place within them but from outside of themselves. The child's behavior isn't changed because they understand it's the better way to behave. They change their behavior because of the carrot or the cookie, the money, or in Helen's case the cake, that is dangled in front of them. Additional misconceptions develop and become reinforced when the one carrot isn't really enough, now the child needs two or more treats before they will comply according to the adults needs and wants and once again, <u>not</u> because they understand it's the right thing to do in that moment. Rewards don't allow the time for a child to want to understand and discern right from wrong. With saucer sized eyes, the child would rather have the treat than to think about what better action to take. In this way, the child learns submission, simple compliance and how to act like a puppet being told when to do something and when not to. In essence they have been robbed of valuable opportunities to think for themselves all for the sake of expediency. They never have to discern right from wrong; why would they when they have someone older and more competent to take care of that for them.

Rewards don't prepare a child for the adult world that they are heading for, and then we, as observers, wonder why adult/children behave the way they do! As they get older the child is presented with more and more challenging social relationship issues. Further along the stages of life, Corporate America wants to know where are the adult/children, the college graduates who can think for themselves.

As the adults in a situation involving a child's bad behavior, it helps to take the time to consider what your real motivations are, as a parent. Is it just a quick fix, an instant remedy you want or is this a valuable teaching moment to instill in the child's character development? What did you want the child to learn? What tool did you help dust off and shine up to present for the child's tool box? What did you want them to walk away with? It would be our parental duty to ask these questions or would it be the parent's reward to just have peace at all cost?

What an easy, instant solution - to use a little bribery for instant parent gratification? With a sigh of relief the problem is resolved. There is no more kicking, screaming, tantrums, hitting, biting - the carrot took care of that! But, by the end of the skirmish what did the child learn? They most likely learned: *'The louder I am, the meaner, and more obnoxious I become, then I'll get a treat, I win a prize. I am rewarded when I'm bad.'*

Kate says: *"There are so many times she simply cannot be compelled."* Miss Annie's response, *"Yes, I'm the same way myself."* How true, even as adults we can be bribed to bribe. Bribery is such an instant fix with no real substance or effort from the parent. What does the child learn? A better question is what does the parent learn? They don't have to rummage around in the tool box for a new tool and discover new alternatives to connect with the child. The parent could come up with an alternative solution resulting in a valuable teaching moment for the child. No, the parent doesn't have to be bothered to take the time. Imagine you as a parent, taking the same amount of time, energy and strategy that Miss Annie took in the next upcoming scene, the breakfast scene. Imagine if every parent took the time, energy and strategy that Miss Annie took in their own home with their own children? What a world this could be!

———

Possible Miracle Worker Dialog – Context Sensitive

Rewarding bad behavior, it happens all the time. Peace at all cost, it happens all the time. What is the message the child learns? What if we were to try to understand what perspective the child is coming from? It doesn't make the behavior right; this is not to condone the behavior. Just take a few minutes to try to understand what is going on in their little head. Clearly they don't feel heard or understood. Ride out the emotion; validate it with some questions...

- *'You seem to be angry!'*
- *'Tell me what's going on.'*
- *'You're behavior tells me you are upset.'*

You will notice that once any of us big or little children feel understood and validated, we ourselves won't need to be on guard to reward or punish behaviors.

———

About punishment - this too, is an external control, not an internal motivator. Probably the biggest misunderstanding comes from the fact that a child, in fact every child/adult child will learn to lie to an adult about whatever is going on so they won't be punished. Children are smart; Helen is very smart. What's also interesting about punishment is the recognition that the child uses the actual punishment and the punisher to be mad at. They totally disregard the inappropriate action they took that brought on the punishment in the first place. The very act of the punishment actually confuses the child. The child does not use this time to process the facts, to have remorse and develop sound character for their behavior, and for the problem. Instead they will become angry with the person who punished them and ultimately blame them. The problem shifted from personal accountability and responsibility to denial and the blame game.

The child's inappropriate reaction to reward and punishment is a very high price to pay. Reward and punishment certainly don't render a speedy recovery to the relationship and the child can and will continue to act out, with no room for growth and maturity. The relationship stays disturbed. Choosing options other than reward and punishment is much preferred. Keep digging in the tool box.

What a Miracle Worker Would Share

Since we were all most likely brought up with some system of rewards and punishment, what are we doing or what are we prevented from doing as adults because we are still waiting for a reward? What is the right thing to do? Do you do it? Or are you waiting for the reward? What lies and fibs have you surrounded yourself with? Are we lying because we fear some sort of retribution which, much like a self-fulfilling prophecy then makes us continue to lie, cheat and take advantage of others? Once we started the lie, the fib, the untruth we can't stop, we have to hold strong to the new 'truth' about the lie, or we will be found out, discovered and reprimanded. We have to dig our heels in and look the individual to whom we are lying right in the eye and continue to lie some more. The stronger you look in their eyes, without blinking, without hesitation - the lie wins; children are very good at this. Adult/children are even better... we have perfected our lies, our look, our insistence. Once you start lying you can't stop for fear of being found out, right?

Could it be time to use that same amount of courage, energy and fortitude it took to lie to begin with, and instead fess up and tell the truth? Either way the consequences are yours to live with. Results can lead to negative consequences with negative karma, 3DL, or you can experience positive consequences with positive karma and be blessed with a life of what some would call 'luck', 4DL. But we all know success doesn't rely solely upon luck. It was the Universe acting as a mirror. The Universe is ready and willing to grant our every wish - both the good wishes and the not-so-good wishes. Whatever we want, whatever we ask for, the Universe is there for us. 3DL or 4DL - the Universe is happy to oblige.

What an amazing view, to sit back a bit and watch the Universe in action. Notice what happens when we make bad choices, when we lie and try to take advantage of others, terrible things happen. Watch your family and friends; check out the neighbors, what goes right in their lives? What doesn't go so right in their lives? When we choose to make better life choices, to listen to our Spirit, to trust the good idea we hear and act on it, life becomes simpler. The ducks are all lined up in a row, the planets are all in line and life seems seamless. We can dig our heels in with honesty, without blinking, without hesitation and lo and behold - the truth wins. What else do we win? We win health, a healthy mind, body and Spirit. We can as a result focus on what is important. We won't have nearly the human drama to weed through to hear our Spirit. We won't have nearly the amount of noise to shut out before we can begin to hear what is really important to us. We can tap into that 95% of the brain we don't use and focus on our Spirit voices, thoughts and great new ideas. We can then begin discovering our passions and make choices to fulfill heartwarming dreams and aspirations; we can live 4DL. We can allow ourselves to trust and believe we will have a life full of blessings with luck on our side. Angels? *"Ahhhh!"*

Life in all its power and possibility can be as easy or as difficult as we make it. Trust that 3DL will be much more difficult than 4DL. Choose daily; choose wisely, every single day. Choose to have a great day or choose to <u>create</u> a great day. Ultimately the choice is always with us. What will you choose to create today?

3DL or 4DL is a choice, which lifestyle do you choose?

Lucky– *Synonyms–*fortunate, opportune, timely, beneficial, good, happy, felicitous, providential, favorable, good omen, promising

OR

Lucky– *Antonyms–*untimely, detrimental, bad, unhappy, unfavorable, unpromising, sinister, ominous

Scene Fourteen

Appropriate or Inappropriate

In this scene the Keller family is sitting together for breakfast. Helen is walking around the table helping herself from everyone's plates and taking any food she wants... with her hands.

Kate: Miss Annie, she's accustomed to helping herself from our plates to anything she---
Miss Annie: Yes, but I'm not accustomed to it.
Captain Keller: Of course not. Viney!
Kate: Jimmy, give her something to quiet her
Brother Jimmy: But her table manners are the best she has.
Captain Keller: Let her this time. It's the only way we get any adult conversation. I'll get you another plate.
Miss Annie: I have a plate, thank you.
Kate: Viney! I'm afraid what Cap'n Keller says is only too true. She'll persist in this until she gets her way.
Miss Annie: I have a plate, nothing's wrong with the plate, I intend to keep it.
Brother Jimmy: You see why they took Vicksburg?
Captain Keller: Miss Sullivan. A plate is no matter to struggle with a deprived child about.
Miss Annie: Oh, I'd sooner have a more heroic issue myself.

The Keller family 'noise' is deafening. Miss Annie realizes being around the family only confuses Helen about the new, more grown up behavior that is expected; even something as simple as sitting together for a family meal is dysfunctional.

Helen has met her match. Statements and excuses like *"she's accustomed to…"* or the comment about the *"deprived child"* is like any parent saying *'She's just a child'* or *'Boys will be boys.'* How many times will the child have their way; *"Let her, this time.",* before a different action is taken demanding a better behavior. What statements are said at your house that allows and tolerates inappropriate behavior? How long do you allow for and tolerate these slips? And then…Boom! Here comes Miss Annie who will not tolerate the behavior, and in fact will not tolerate any of their behaviors. Not the Captain's, the Mother's the Brother's and especially not Helen's.

———

Possible Miracle Worker Dialog—Context Sensitive

Brother Jimmy goes a little political here: *"You see why they took Vicksburg?* Captain Keller adds: *"A plate is no matter to struggle with a deprived child about."*

How are your children at the dinner table? Appropriate or inappropriate? Are they set up for success, or for failure? What does your child need to have so the family can enjoy a nice family dinner together? First, be sure they are being fed on a child's schedule and not on the adult schedule. At the very least have some snack type appetizer to satisfy possible sugar dips and mood swings.

Then there are the days when you plan to go out for dinner. How do you prepare for an outing with your children? Here are some pointed questions to ask the children so they will know exactly what to expect.

-*'So what kind of behavior do we have when we go out to eat?'* Let the child respond.
-*'What kind of manners do we have at a restaurant?'* Let the child respond.
-*'Do we walk or run around the restaurant?'* Let the child respond.
-*'What voice do we use when we are at the restaurant?'* Let the child respond.
-*'What do we say to the waiter, waitress when they serve us?'* Let the child respond…

If the responses are not appropriate respond with *'So you don't want to go out with us?'* Be sure to leave an opportunity for the child to change their mind especially when you encourage *'We certainly will miss you.'* Be sure to follow up the above questions with *'What if…?'* For example: *'What should happen if you get cranky or tired while we are out?'* Let the child respond. Brainstorm ideas, pulling from the child. Be sure to let them know you are prepared to let the waitress pack up the food and bring it home. Of course how you react if you really have to pack up the dinner to leave is the key to success. If you provide the child with a button-pushing opportunity by showing your anger disappointment or despair, well you know - children love to push buttons! You may also want to do a practice run at a time when you would be fine with walking out of the restaurant if you had to. You will find you may not have to leave the restaurant often when the child(ren) understand expectations.

One of the best opportunities for having a conversation with your child(ren) about expectations when they arrive at a restaurant, the zoo, grandma's house, the park or church, is while driving in the car. This is an excellent time to follow through with the cranky, tired dinner example; the same expectations apply. Remember, leaving is the key to thwarting wayward behaviors.

———

At this point in the story Miss Annie is certainly someone to dislike. Miss Annie has dared to call everyone out on their tolerance of Helen's inappropriate behavior, at the dining table just so the family can have *"adult conversation"*. Change has to come to all if real change is to take hold and last. Clearly the family standards need to be raised. For the Keller family members, each and everyone will have to realize how their interactions with Helen only perpetuate the negative behaviors a child - any child, should have outgrown. Miss Annie has to stand firm in her convictions and use these everyday interactions as the primer for Helen. Before Miss Annie is able to reach Helen on an internal level, there is a need to establish enough decorum from the family members and especially from Helen. Miss Annie will not have any success with Helen if all this external family drama continues unfettered.

"The family naturally felt inclined to interfere, especially her father,
who cannot bear to see her cry.
So they were all willing to give in for the sake of peace. Besides, her past
experiences and associations were all against me. I saw clearly that it was
useless to try to teach her language or anything else until
she learned to obey me."

Story of My Life, Annie Sullivan p256

What a Miracle Worker Would Share

Certainly the breakfast scene was extremely trying for Miss Annie, but she risks the rejection - she doesn't even know Helen enough to feel rejected. Although, if we think about it, and consciously connect for a moment, Miss Annie had the most to lose if she were rejected; she loses her job. Now there's a reason not to speak up, risking the job and staying co-dependent. How many times do we bite our tongue instead of saying the needed comment due to fear of losing a job, maybe a promotion? Miss Annie rode a train all the way from Massachusetts. We already know that this is Miss Annie's first job. I'd say she risks an enormous amount if she were rejected. But if she didn't risk and didn't speak up, what kind of positive influence could Miss Annie encourage? If parents don't risk and don't speak up, what kind of positive influence could be encouraged? Not much. And then comes the chaos and various dysfunctions that have to be tolerated or handled. There's that family noise again.

Every family has family noise. The use of excuses, manipulations and enablement is synonymous with 'family noise'. Such a distraction really – it's so unfortunate that so many families tolerate and believe that the family noise is just the way it is. Although…hmmm… if we thought about it, maybe family noise is really a great gauge. It is this exact noise, this exact degree of noise that we could use in order to discern that a different action needs to be taken. One of the tools in your tool box is available to do the complete opposite of whatever strategy you are currently using. If you are tolerating behaviors and it creates family noise and 3DL dysfunction, then we know we have to do the complete opposite action which is to not tolerate these behaviors.

We can choose to deal with the family noise now, or deal with it later. At some point the Universe will be sure to help us realize we cannot wait any longer. The situation becomes out of hand, it is so grave and the consequence so dear. As mentioned before, *'Life can be as easy or as difficult as we make it. When we choose to make better life choices, to listen to our Spirit, trust what we hear and act on it, life is simpler.'* So maybe it would be better to deal now! Angels are full of hope... *"Ahhhh!"*

3DL or 4DL is a choice, which lifestyle do you choose?

Tolerate– *Synonyms–*bear, endure, put up with, stand, take, suffer, abide, stomach, allow, permit, let, sanction, consent to, admit, recognize,

OR

Tolerate– *Antonyms–*forbid, prohibit, disallow, outlaw, ban, prevent, oppose

Scene Fifteen

Teachable Moment

This is the famous breakfast scene where Miss Annie insists that Helen learn manners at the dining table. Miss Annie challenges Helen's will and doesn't give up. This is a pivotal moment for little Helen.

Captain Keller: No, I really must insist you...now, she's hurt herself.
Miss Annie: No, she hasn't.
Captain Keller: Will you please let her hands go?
Kate: Miss Annie, You don't know the child well enough yet, she'll keep--...
Miss Annie: I know an ordinary tantrum well enough, when I see one and a badly spoiled child.
Brother Jimmy: Hear, hear.
Captain Keller: Miss Sullivan! You'd have more understanding of your pupil if you had some pity in you. Now kindly do as I--.
Miss Annie: Pity? For this tyrant? The whole house turns on her whims. Is there anything she wants she doesn't get? I'll tell you what I pity, that the sun won't rise and set for her all her life and everyday you're telling her it will. What good will your pity do when you're gone?
Captain Keller: Kate, for the love of heaven will you...
Kate: Miss Annie, please, I don't think it serves to lose our...
Miss Annie: Serves you good. It's less trouble to feel sorry for her than to teach her anything better, isn't it?
Captain Keller: I fail to see where you have taught her anything yet Miss Sullivan!
Miss Annie: I'll begin now if you leave the room, Captain Keller!
Captain Keller: Leave?
Miss Annie: Everyone, please!
Captain Keller: Miss Sullivan, you are a paid teacher, nothing more.

Miss Annie*: I can't unteach her six years of pity if you can't stand up to one tantrum! Old Stonewall indeed! Mrs. Keller, you promised me help. Leave me alone with her now.*

Imagine being Miss Annie for a moment, she just witnessed an incredible dysfunctional family meal time and the adults in the room thought it was perfectly fine, normal and acceptable. Here's how Miss Annie felt:

> *"Helen's table manners are appalling. She put her hands in our plates and helps herself, and when the dishes are passed, she grabs them and takes out whatever she wants.*
> *This morning I wouldn't let her put her hand in my plate. She persisted and a contest of wills followed. Naturally the family was much disturbed, and left the room. I locked the dining-room door, and proceeded to eat my breakfast, though the food almost choked me.*
> *Helen was lying on the floor, kicking and screaming and trying to pull my chair from under me. She kept this up for half an hour, then she got up to see what I was doing. I let her see that I was eating, but I did not let her put her hand in the plate. She pinched me and I slapped her every time she did it. Then she went all round the table to see who was there, and finding no one but me, she seemed bewildered. After a few minutes she came back to her place and began to eat her breakfast with her fingers. I gave her a spoon, which she threw on the floor. I forced her out of the chair and made her pick it up. Finally I succeeded in getting her back in her chair again and held the spoon in her hand, compelling her to take up the food with it and put it in her mouth. In a few minutes she yielded and finished her breakfast peaceable. Then we had another tussle over folding her napkin. When she had finished she threw it on the floor and ran toward the door. Finding it locked, she began to kick and scream all over again. It was another hour before I succeeded in getting her napkin folded. Then I let her out into the warm sunshine and went up to my room and threw myself on the bed exhausted. I had a good cry and felt better. I suppose I shall have many such battles with the little woman before she learns the only two essential things I can teach her, obedience and love."*
> **Annie Sullivan, Story of My Life, p255.**

Let's pick apart some of the favorite phrases in this dinner interlude. Actually, here are some of Miss Annie's greatest moments. Miss Annie has to fight off the enabling dad. *"She's hurt herself."* Or worse, *"You'd have more understanding if you had some pity."* Go Miss Annie… *"Pity? For this tyrant? The whole house turns on her whims."* Amen, finally someone, someone on the outside of the family, a third party member has shared with the Kellers the truth of what is really going on in the family.

Pity creates more tyranny. *"What good will your pity do when you're gone?"* Go Miss Annie! What does pity do for your child? Maybe they are too fat, too short, don't have a mother, don't have a father, look funny, have a disability; maybe they are a slow learner, or worse a drug addict, an alcoholic, anorexic. How is this pity creating tyranny in your home? What would a third party member discover about your household… if they were invited in?

Push for a more personal example, maybe there is a teacher that your child can't stand and rejects. Why? Is this the teacher that really challenges the child, the teacher that really understands the character traits that need improvement? Maybe it was a sports coach or scout leader. Child advocates usually try to make a difference in children's lives. All child-based programs, schools, teams and scouting programs help your child to get along with others. Did you rescue the situation by removing the child? The Miss Annie's of the world would respond: *"Is there anything she doesn't get? What I pity is that the sun won't rise and set for her, and you're telling her it will. What good will your pity do when you're gone?"*

Especially poignant is Miss Annie's response: *"It's less trouble to feel sorry than to teach her anything."* How true this comment is for the majority of families today, because it is far less trouble to feel sorry than to take the time to teach. Taking the time to teach someone can easily become overwhelming and tiresome. It definitely takes effort. Look at the amount of effort Miss Annie demonstrated just in this breakfast scene. It's far easier for the parent to send the child to school and hope the child will learn manners from a teacher, as if, somehow it's in the teachers job description to teach manners. It is so much easier to have the child out of your hair by sending them off to camp, than it is to take the time to discipline your own child. Where else could you send the child?

Symbolically, how many more personal breakfast scenes do you need to act out until the Universe stops with these repetitive life lessons over and over again until you finally 'get it'? When will you eat with a spoon and fold your napkin? Folded napkins and eating with a spoon are some of the rudimentary but necessary steps to take before hopes and dreams can be realized. Miss Annie knows this and expects these baby steps from Helen.

——⁓⦿⦿⦿⦿⦿⁓——

Possible Miracle Worker Dialog—Context Sensitive

Mom and toddler celebrated yesterday. How clever the child was, having put on her own socks and shoes. Maybe the baby isn't a baby anymore. Uh-oh! What's happening today? The toddler is having a tantrum because she can't quite manage to get her socks and shoes on. Yesterday she could and today she can't? Mom ponders for a moment that it would be easier for her to just put them on herself so they can go about their day. Certainly the toddler would quit her fussing; Mom could enable the situation and therefore wouldn't have to listen to the noise anymore. What would the child learn? *'If I complain enough, Mom will always fix the problem.'* Would this be 3DL or 4DL? What would 4DL look like in a situation like this? Mom could encourage…

Mom: *Honey, try again. You're clever; I know you will figure it out!* Mom walks away.
Child: Louder tantrum ensues as if being louder, sadder, more frustrated will rope Mom in to fix the problem. Being louder and madder always works! At least it used to!
Mom: Keep walking; don't let the inappropriate tantrum behavior be a reason to discipline too. What do you want to accomplish? Don't get confused in the moment. Yes, the tantrum is inappropriate and maybe even more so now that you have walked away. We are working on encouraging the child to put on her socks and shoes right now. We can deal with the tantrum later.

——⁓⦿⦿⦿⦿⦿⁓——

This may seem like a small step, maybe even too small to bother with. Consider the importance of these small steps mastered which give the child the important tools they will need in the future. It is small steps like these that can become building blocks for achieving bigger life issues in the future. If we let the child 'off the hook' for such a small task, they won't learn the feeling and importance of dedicated effort to overcome daily obstacles that may seem small to someone else, but are none the less a big task for a little person. If we let this small task slide by, what would be the next situation we would let slide, and then the next and the next. This pattern of rescuing doesn't make for independent, self reliant or autonomous individuals. Nevertheless, we insist upon rescuing all because we wanted to be the competent giant in our child's life, all because we didn't want to deal, all because we didn't want to hear the noise.

The Kellers didn't deal with the very small step of teaching table manners to Helen. Take these small steps as very valuable teaching moments, all designed to build up to the larger steps in life. Be adamant in the behavior you expect of your child. They will take these lessons into their adult lives. Give your child boundaries, limits, protocol and the understanding that there are certain appropriate ways to behave with manners at the top of the list. If you don't teach them, who will?

Captain Keller is so ready to dismiss Miss Annie, the change agent. He doesn't want to hear the noise as if somehow Helen is being hurt by simply asking her to behave. Notice Captain Keller's very 'noisy' response; *"You are a paid teacher, nothing more."* Now there's a statement which would make anyone feel like they should slow down feeling threatened about losing their job. Who knows what the Kellers expected from Miss Annie? Who knows what you as a parent expect from those who are with your child when they are out of the house? Did Captain Keller really expect Miss Annie to be like them? Did they want just another person in the house to show pity and enable Helen? It's pretty clear the pity and enablement showered upon Helen hasn't worked.

What A Miracle Worker Would Share

Why would you tolerate inappropriate behaviors? Not that rejection stuff again. Maybe the following quote from Miss Annie will shine some light on why we wouldn't want to tolerate certain behaviors. The best part about this quote is in understanding that Helen had rages early on as her primary form of communication. With Miss Annie's help and perseverance Helen was finally heard and understood and eventually given some valuable tools to help make a big difference in her life. When Helen dug in her tool box and used the shiny cleaned up tools and life skills Miss Annie taught her - only then did Helen's training turn her life into *"organized power"*.

"Her early rages were an unhappy expression of the natural force of character with instruction as to turn into trained and organized power."
Story of My Life, Annie Sullivan p342.

Of course, it's easier to pity a child rather than to insist upon and be adamant about better behavior. The parent may risk feeling rejected from the child, especially if the altercation is trying, and a true test of wills. Notice how you in particular would respond or not respond maybe because you wouldn't want to rock the boat and have anyone mad at you. This situation happens whether you are responding to a child, a family member, a co-worker or a spouse. Notice the hesitation to do the right thing and actually take an appropriate action to better the situation at hand. This may take some reflection, but honestly ask yourself why you didn't take action. Are you ready to let the *"natural forces of character"*, with instruction, turn into trained and organized power for your child? Are you ready to empower your child, risk the relationship, or hide behind the fears of being rejected?

What is the result of pity? What does an individual learn if someone pities them? Let's think for a moment of a memory you have where someone enabled you and had pity for you? Did you walk away feeling empowered or did you have a sense of desiring more pity or maybe even enjoying the pity, after all, you do get a lot of attention from being pitied. What is ever asked of you if you demonstrate the need for pity? Nothing is asked of you. Why would anyone ask you to do anything, you couldn't possibly do it anyway so we'll just avoid the obvious rather than push the obvious. Is this what Helen learned? *'Anything goes, I'm not capable so I don't even have to try, but boy I sure do get attention from well meaning people who want to do things for me. Why should I do anything, there's always someone to do them for me!'*

Miss Annie clearly knows what she's up against. Miss Annie doesn't just have to teach Helen, she has to teach all the Kellers - the entire family! If the extended Keller family can't put their full weight behind Miss Annie, Miss Annie doesn't have much of a chance. Go Annie! Stick to your beliefs, stick to your methods, and be adamant about your formula for success. Angels *"Ahhhh!"*

Oh yes, and about the teacher's job description mentioned earlier... maybe a teacher needs to send an unruly child home. The unruly child is the child who steals the time, energy and freedom away from the rest of the students who are there to learn, who are there being in their Spirit. If the child is sent home the parent becomes automatically enrolled in an immediate Life Skills course before the child can come back to class. It is the parent's obligation to instill inner discipline in the child, the better behavior expected. Certainly this would help reduce the teacher's time from having to spend every two to three minutes managing the inappropriate behavior in the classroom. Don't be fooled, this is exactly how much time a teacher is normally spending on managing classroom behavior, and on many occasions it may be even more than that. Is your child being robbed because of inappropriate behavior in the classroom? More importantly, unless the parent wants to experience a natural consequence of having to enroll in a Life Skills course, the parent would take the parental steps necessary to redirect their child's behavior so as not to be disturbed from their daily work schedules. Angels would agree... *"Ahhhh!"*

3DL or 4DL is a choice, which lifestyle do you choose?

Adamant— *Synonyms*—insistent, unyielding, inflexible, rigid, fixed, set, firm, tough, immovable, unbending, resolute, determined, stubborn

OR

Adamant— *Antonym*—yielding, flexible, lax, undemanding, easy-going, indifferent, submissive, capitulating, compliant

Scene Sixteen

Overcoming Frustrations

In this scene, Captain Keller is outraged by Miss Annie's unconventional behavior toward his daughter Helen. He is ready to fire her.

Captain Keller: *Katie, come outside with me at once!*
Miss Annie: *Out, please.*
Brother Jimmy: *If it takes all summer, General! (Annie slams the door, locks it and takes the key)*
Captain Keller: *I've a mind to ship her back to Boston, and you can inform her so for me!*
Kate: *I, Cap'n?*
Captain Keller: *She's a hireling. Now I want it clear, unless there's an apology and complete change of manner, she goes back on the next train! Will you make that clear?*
Kate: *Where will you be, Cap'n, while I am making it clear?*
Captain Keller: *At the office.*
Brother Jimmy: *Will you? I thought what she said was exceptionally intelligent. I've been sayin' it for years.*
Kate: *To his face? Or will you take it, Jimmy, as a flag?*

Let's take another important look at the role Brother Jimmy plays. Jimmy represents that individual in the home that is contrary to the beliefs that currently exist in the family. Jimmy sees life a little differently. It seems Jimmy actually sees and thinks much more like Miss Annie. He was the 'Miss Annie' in the family before Miss Annie even came into the Keller household; he just didn't know how to be adamant enough to be heard, yet! Both Jimmy and Miss Annie are examples of the ones you can both love and hate in the family, because both of them go against the grain; they both tell the truth. How sad to think, telling the truth goes against the grain! In the pecking order of the typical family they are the family members who are not co-dependent to the same degree as the other family members, and they are definitely not the enablers. They don't cross the very delicate line between helping and over helping; enabling. They are easy to dislike within the family; they are easily made out to be the scapegoat and are usually considered the black sheep of the family. The truth about these family members who speak honestly - they represent the voice of integrity, the clear thinking we know we should embody; they are the truth-sayers.

These Miss Annie 'types' that live in the family have the most difficulty in being heard, especially since their voices goes against the current family belief systems (BS). They try and try again without much success. As difficult as it is to hang tough in their beliefs, they are the only ones contrary to the rest of the family's beliefs. This doesn't make them wrong; it just feels like they are walking a different path, a path that feels foreign to the rest of the family. They stray away from the family's ideals and no one else is comfortable with these newer, different beliefs so, *'They just have to be wrong! Right?'* These contrary beliefs force the other members of the family to face looking outside of their comfort levels where it is most often too difficult to look; they are out of their comfort zones. These opposing family members virtually gang up against the voice of reason, the voice of right and better thinking. An uncomfortable place to be, nevertheless they continue to try and make a difference because they know it's the right thing to do.

> *"...and nobody had ever seriously disputed her will, except occasionally her brother James, until I came; and like all tyrants she holds tenaciously to her divine right to do as she pleases."*
> **Annie Sullivan, Story of My Life p256**

Didn't the Kellers try to find someone to make a difference for Helen? Well, that usually means a different teaching approach, which usually means trying an opposite technique. If this is true, certainly doing anything opposite would feel very foreign, uncomfortable and out of the ordinary comfort zone for the Kellers. Amazingly and sadly, there seems to be a better chance of 'hearing the message' from a family outsider instead of from a blood relative. Any family members that attempt to make an honest difference are usually shot down. Families typically want to simply shoot the messenger; they don't want to hear it, and they don't want to know. How long will these messengers hang around in this dysfunctional and sometimes very toxic environment, waiting for change to happen? These scapegoats eventually escape. They are making the effort to live, or at least straddle, the 4DL with the 3DL. Once you understand and recognize the bigger picture of the Universe's plan, it's difficult, uncomfortable and toxic to go back and remain in 3DL.

There are two concepts to review in this scene. First, who in your family is the Miss Annie, the one who tells the truth and is made out to be the scapegoat, all because the family couldn't handle the truth? Secondly, who is the tyrant in your home that *"...holds tenaciously to their divine right to do as they please"*? This individual is the stuck-in-the-mud, unhealthy individual who has burrowed in and won't let up on the brakes at all. Most likely the tyrant in your home is the individual who everyone else pities the most. Be it drugs, alcohol, crime issues, or health issues, due to the typical text-book family pecking order, there is an individual in your home who embodies this role. The rest of the family members all pull out the violins and the family orchestra play quite a high pitch squeaky and nasty version of a pity-party. This is text-book too!

Brother Jimmy 'sees' much like Miss Annie sees. Both Miss Annie and Jimmy come from and understand EQ - the Emotional Quotient or Emotional Intelligence of the situation. Some of us have more EQ than others - a common sense, if you will. Some of us reveal an intelligence that understands the social and emotional responses needed to better cope with the daily demands of life. The rest of us could learn a great deal more about Emotional Intelligence in order to discover additional 'common sense' tools, thereby making life so much easier.

What a Miracle Worker Would Share

What is amazing about the many Brother Jimmies and Miss Annies of the world is there does come a time when they finally get the other family members to admit to the family dysfunction. It's their job, their role in the family to shine that special light. Then finally, the other family members admit everything; the family dysfunction, their part in the dysfunction and how tired they are with the current family standard. Finally they are tired of the chaos. Finally their minds can no longer fool their hearts. They may not be real clear about what to do next, but they are open and ready to take off the brakes and ask for help. Most phenomenal and gallant is the initial courage of the first family member who actually breaks the mold and says out loud; *'How did you know?'* and *'What do we do about it?'* Angels… *"Ahhhh!"*

—⁓◦◦◎⊙⊙◎◦◦⁓—

Possible Miracle Worker Dialog- Context Sensitive

The Brother Jimmies and Miss Annies often take the opportunities presented to them and stand up for raised standards. They fearlessly speak up and risk telling the truth. It's as if these incredibly courageous family members make imaginary check marks in the air with their finger, but only if they have been able to 'shake up' family members with the apparent new world view. The check marks are mental notes in the air as if to say, *'Good, they are mad. I have shaken them up. They are finally considering that life could be different. They have been shaken up with a whole different paradigm to consider!'*

The more imaginary check marks created in the air the better. This is uncomfortable, even out of the norm, but the Brother Jimmies and Miss Annies do it anyway because it's important and something they have seriously considered important to share. We love and honor family enough to do and say the hard thing. They champion the will of the one's they love. Most importantly, don't ever think for a moment that it is easy to tell the truth and risk the relationship for the change agent. Risking the family relationship may be forever!

—⁓◦◦◎⊙⊙◎◦◦⁓—

If you think about it, this is not much different than the times when you grabbed your child's hand out of the cookie jar and exclaimed *'Dinner will be ready in ten minutes! You can have a cookie after dinner.'* The child will not like this and may even be mad at you. As a parent you do it anyway because it's the right thing to do. Miss Annie is doing nothing more than grabbing Helen's hand out of the cookie jar. Miss

Annie is doing nothing more than taking Captain Keller's hand out of the cookie jar. Miss Annie is doing nothing more than taking Brother Jimmie's hand out of the cookie jar and the same for Aunt Ev and Kate. *'No cookies 'til after dinner! And that's final.'*

As a family member or as a friend in the role as the change agent, the individual or individuals you interact with may be initially mad at you, but you shared the truth anyway because it's the right thing to do. You may risk the relationship in the process, but you know you are being of real service. You are not beating around the bush, telling half-truths, nor are you tip-toeing around the obvious realities. No, you are straightforward, honest and reflect as a true friend or family member. You are of genuine service. Anything else is just a farce within the relationship; anything else is disingenuous and self serving.

Of course, sharing truths could be the norm if more of us would courageously and fearlessly do it! The risk wouldn't be so grand if more of us would courageously and fearlessly do it! The shock wouldn't be so overwhelming, if more of us would courageously and fearlessly do it! We could change the norm of not sharing truths to actively sharing the truth, if more of us courageously and fearlessly shared the truth. Imagine what a world we could be! Live fearlessly, be of service and take risks. Angels… *"Ahhhh!"*

3DL or 4DL is a choice, which lifestyle do you choose?

Courageous– *Synonyms*–brave, valiant, bold, fearless, dauntless, strong hearted, unafraid, chivalrous, manly, dashing, gallant, bold-spirited, heroic.

OR

Courageous– *Antonyms*–cowardly, fainthearted, timid, fearful, apprehensive.

Scene Seventeen

Helen Has Met Her Match

This is the famous breakfast scene in the Helen Keller story; Miss Annie insists that Helen eat with a fork! The rest of the family waits outside. If at all possible, be sure to watch the original video on this part of the movie. (Search *YouTube* for the full showing of <u>The Miracle Worker</u>.)

(banging) (makes guttural sounds) (stamps feet)
Miss Annie*: Good girl, Helen. Agh!*
Aunt Ev*: I don't see how you can wait here a minute longer, Kate. This could go on all afternoon too.*
Kate*: I'll tell the Cap'n you called.*
Viney*: Give me her, Miss Kate. I'll sneak her in back to her crib.*
Kate*: This child never gives me a minute's worry.*
Viney*: Oh, yes. This one's the angel of the family. No question about that.*

Have you ever been in a position such as Miss Annie? Have you ever needed to fearlessly insist on a certain belief and have others buy into or agree with this alternative position? Of course you have. Every day we communicate with other individuals. Every day we're busy trying to explain a belief, an idea, a new concept, or a system unique to anyone who doesn't yet *know*.

To *know* is the operative word. Maybe you don't *know* about the early bird special and you didn't qualify for the discounts. Maybe you don't *know* about the sale special and the special only applies to… Did you get mad, ask questions or insist on an explanation? Maybe there was some fine print that wasn't read or for that matter even seen. I'm sure you didn't take the news too well. Helen doesn't take the news well either but Miss Annie needs to insist that Helen follow her rules. Without these rules Helen would be enabled and allowed to continue behaving as she normally does. For seven years Helen has lived a life of total dysfunction, living permissibly with minimal limits or structured boundaries. Helen would need a strong personality to challenge her and to totally flip her belief system around. Someone who wouldn't let her get her way with inappropriate behavior, someone who would champion her will.

Helen needed to *know* there was only one acceptable way to behave if she were in Miss Annie's presence. Helen needed to understand Miss Annie's expectations and standards. Helen needed to *know* she wouldn't 'get away' with her inappropriate behaviors. Appropriate or Inappropriate? Helen for once in her life needed to *know* that there is difference. There was a new standard established by Miss Annie and Helen needed to *know* Miss Annie would 'catch' her and not let her fall below these standards. Miss Annie was effectively teaching Helen and demanded that Helen have a certain amount of expected behavior and decorum. Not until Helen understood the new ground rules would she be able to take the *next step* with Miss Annie, or in life.

> *"I have thought about it a great deal, and the more I think, the more certain I am that obedience is the gateway through which knowledge, yes, and love, too, enter the mind of the child."*
> **Annie Sullivan, The Story of My Life p257**

Miss Annie *knows*. Miss Annie understood that only by teaching Helen behavioral manners and expecting a certain amount of decorum could Helen then actually begin to learn. When Helen was so busy tied up with inappropriate drama type behavior, Miss Annie knew she would never be able to reach Helen's core to even pose a question about what she wanted out of life. Without being quiet, calm enough and in her Spirit, Helen would never be able to consider her life options. We ourselves often become too wrapped up in the negative energies of life to allow ourselves to discover the positive energies of life. The negatives keep us busy, so busy that we don't even have the ability to consider how exciting life could be.

How different and wonderful life could become. Much like a tornado spiral, we have the choice of spiraling downward toward more negative experiences or deciding upon different choices so that a positive upward spiral of experience would be possible. This can only be possible when we tap into and develop our inner discipline to be in the *know*.

Helen is no different than the rest of us. She has her story and we have our story. We all struggle with life choices. If there is no one, especially a parent to teach and guide, how would we *know* how to behave? How would we *know* life could be as easy or as hard as we choose and create it?

What are the rules of life? Without rules we would experience quite the chaotic life, a life full of anarchy. Helen didn't have rules, didn't *know* there were rules and her life was indeed chaotic. Let's take a look at an example of a freshman student entering College, maybe you had this experience. Here you are young and fresh out of high school embarking on a new adventure. As a fresh-man, you go to the campus, don't *know* where to go or what to do. There are rules, systems, and protocol that haven't been taught or communicated to you yet. Fortunately, you can communicate and ask questions. Fortunately you can actually see the individual to whom you would ask a question to. Your enrollment day might prove frustrating upon realizing you stood in a line you didn't need to stand in for two hours. By the end of the day however you have a better grasp on how the system works. You start to connect to what is expected of you. Next semester will run so much smoother because - now you *know*.

Unfortunately, Helen had no tools. Consequences were also difficult for a deaf and blind child to connect with. Helen *knows* she didn't get her way often, which was most likely her biggest life consequence since there was no one to teach or guide her as to the whys, especially the reason why life didn't work out for her. We can only imagine Helen's frustrations. Of course, Helen doesn't *know* any different but how did she learn to meet everyday necessary needs like being hungry, learning about toilet needs, or how to communicate that she's not feeling well?

Helen had to learn that a dysfunctional, 3DL drama-filled life doesn't work for her anymore, and will no longer be tolerated. Miss Annie *knows* she needs Helen to behave in order to reach her. Miss Annie *knows* she needs to reach her Spirit, to reach Helen on an internal level. At the same time Helen needs to experience consequences. For example, when Helen finishes getting dressed then she can eat breakfast. Helen needed first to understand that this new strategy being asked of her was something to be mastered before she could participate in this new and better version of the game of life.

> *"And right here I want to say something which is for your ears alone. Something within me tells me that I shall succeed beyond my dreams. Were it not for some circumstances that make such an idea highly improbable, even absurd. I should think Helen's education would surpass in interest and wonder Dr. Howe's achievement. I know that she has remarkable powers, and I believe that I shall be able to develop and mould them. I cannot tell you how I know these things. I had no idea a short time ago how to go to work; I was feeling about in the dark; but somehow I know now, and I know that I know. I cannot explain it; but when difficulties arise, I am not perplexed or doubtful. I know I meet them; I seem to Divine Helen's peculiar needs. It is wonderful."*
> **Annie Sullivan, Story of My Life. p 275**

This was the day! As Miss Annie was on a roll in reaching Helen's Spirit, Miss Annie *knows* she needed to remove any and all distractions that would impede the progress thus far. Miss Annie already summed up the family dynamics enough to *know* that Helen remaining in the presence of her family would only provide Helen with the same unproductive results. *This was the day.* This was the day that everything in the Keller household would change. This was the day; the Kellers could no longer deny the inevitable. This was the day the family would admit change was upon them and begin to accept the change. Success would depend on everyone being able to tolerate the uncomfortable feeling and discomforts change brings about.

It's important here to note Kate's conversation with Viney, the housekeeper. As Mom continues to wait outside, Viney takes Helen's baby sister for her nap.

Viney: Give me her, Miss Kate. I'll sneak her in back to her crib.
Kate: She never gives me a minute's worry.
Viney: Oh, yes. This one's the angel of the family. No question about that.

Every family does this; they label the children within the family, the pecking order. Each member in the family will have different labels:
-'The angel of the family.' - as we saw in *The Miracle Worker.*
-'The studious one, I find her up at midnight still reading.'
-The rebellious one, the bad one, the pretty one, the black sheep, the athlete.

How does a young child earn this reputation already? What behaviors demonstrate the final 'label' and belief about any child? Is this a healthy belief? As a parent what could you do in order to provide a better balance for the child? Watch which way the pendulum swings, for example: For the studious child, don't always bring home the expected book as a gift. What would be the opposite? What about a board game so the child is encouraged to be with others, instead of the typical response of withdrawing with a book? For the rebellious child, focus on what they do right, which would be the opposite of constantly collecting evidence about what is wrong with them. Draw out the appropriate moments rather than the inappropriate. Make comments about what they are doing, especially when you can see that they really are enjoying what it is they are doing. Even more important, stop what you are doing and take some time to visit with the child when they are involved with an activity and totally self-involved. Meet them with the same emotions they are showing. Comment upon how amazing their 'project' looks. Let them know you wish you could do that, and maybe they could show or teach you sometime.

—ᴠᴠᴠ·ᴏᴇᴪᴏᴏᴪᴇᴏᴏᴠᴠᴠ—

Possible Miracle Worker Dialog - Context Sensitive

For the angel or the good child in the family, tell them to bring you home a detention!? Unconventional, definitely something Miss Annie, a miracle worker, would do. Consider letting them experience 'survival' for their supposedly naughty behavior from authority figures. Help them to loosen up, help them to be less rigid or afraid…

Parent: 'Honey, you know what I would like you to do?'
Child: 'What?' Cringing not knowing what to expect.
Parent: 'I would like you to bring home a detention from school.'
Child: Staring in total disbelief.
Parent: 'I've been noticing that you seem to be scared that you might get into trouble, as if you were doing something wrong. You might do things wrong and I bet you wouldn't do it on purpose. I'm thinking you should do something wrong on purpose, get a detention so you can realize it's not so terrible if you make a mistake and have to go to the principal's office.'
Child: Still staring in disbelief with a look of –Oh no, I could never do that!
Parent: 'Yes, that's what I would like you to do *and* I'm thinking we should have a party when you bring home the detention. We need to celebrate that it's ok for someone to think you are bad and that you did something bad. Right now you are so afraid you can't even be yourself. I want you to learn that it's ok to make mistakes.'
Child: The daughter leaves thinking it over with continued disbelief and believing she could never do that.

Fast forward three weeks.

Child: Comes running to the car line with her best friend Maggie with her beautiful head of red hair. She pops open the car door, hopping up and down, gleefully yelling out. 'Mom, I got a detention!'
Parent: 'Wow, let me see. Congratulations! We have to celebrate, we need to have party!'
Maggie: Looking right at the parent—'Oh my, could you tell that to my parents?!'
Parent: 'Oh no Maggie, it would never work at your house.'
Maggie: 'It wouldn't, why not?'
Parent: 'Oh Maggie, because you get too many detentions!' (Something about that red hair!)

Now this is a very opposite-thinking kind of approach and used only for the child who is so shy, rigid and afraid of taking and making the wrong move. They can't move to the right or to the left without being afraid. How would you unwind them, relax them, and help them to be less anxious, less co-dependent? Think about this one and see the miracle that could be experienced for the child with this type of temperament. Let them experience the reality that they will survive and they are not 'bad'. Help them to be in their Spirit and not solely in the adults' and authorities' Spirit. Of course, this would not necessarily be the strategy to use for the rebellious child. It is important to assess and discern what is best for each individual child. One strategy you would use on one child may very well backfire on another child. Read them, read their energy, see them, understand them and then diligently choose a special strategy for the particular child and the particular situation in mind.

Are you ready for the next step? How do you get to the *knowing* of what to do with your child, with your life or with anything? How do you balance your child's pendulum of life? When the pendulum is swinging from one side to the next, what's a parent to do to best guide a child? How will you reach within yourself to that internal place for answers and actually act on it?

Notice first and foremost that the solutions are different for each individual. For the one who withdraws, you would need to recognize and create more participation type of opportunities so they won't always be by themselves or feel alone. For the one who seeks inappropriate attention you could find ways to honor when they are by themselves, enjoying being self-involved. Like an old fashioned weight scale, balance the needs of each individual. After all, the needs are different; therefore the strategy must be different. Take the time to find the balance. Respect their individuality; reach them at their individual level. Enough of these cookie cutter, one-size-fits-all kids, we are all different and should be reached and guided as such. Yes - this may take more time, initially, but the results are very well worth the effort. Each child needs to *know* and understand that it's not so important to be just like everyone else. We must honor and celebrate their individuality so that they will explore their passions and gifts as the unique individuals they are, and not try to be someone or something they are not.

"There isn't a living soul in this part of the world to whom I can go for advice in this or indeed, in any other education difficulty. The only thing for me to do in a perplexity is to go ahead and learn by making mistakes."
Annie Sullivan, Story of My Life. P283

What a Miracle Worker Would Share

Here's another strategy you may want to try... although it might be a mistake!!! Discern for yourself who in your family could use this strategy. What a brilliant and fascinating opportunity presenting itself when the 'good' child says a 'bad' word. Yes, a <u>bad</u> word. Consider this strategy, unorthodox maybe, but something Miss Annie would have done...

So, the child has just said a bad word! Recalling, you realize it's not the first time. Seems throughout the week certain words have been whispered and even mumbled by the child... since the child already knows saying a bad word is inappropriate. Thank goodness for that! Whispering back, ask the child if they want to play the 'bad word game.' *'Would you like to play the bad word game with me?'* Eagerly, they will want to play, what child wouldn't want to play a game? Ask them, *'What is your favorite bad word?'* The child will be stunned and shocked. Play with this unconventional strategy... where is the child's pendulum? Help them to swing the pendulum along for a better balance in their lives. Notice the change from rigid to relieved and much more relaxed??? Watch their little faces when you give a 'bad' behavior a special place to be explored, a virtual place of permission.

Initial reactions would be one of doubt, *'I'll be in trouble if I say a bad word.'* So, you'll have to encourage them to say the bad word, still in a whisper. *'I know you know bad words, you must have a favorite bad word.'* Finally they realize they can really play with you and not get in trouble for tepidly being a little bit bad. Dialog could look like: *'Wow that is a bad word, is that your favorite bad word?'* Still whispering, *'Do you have another favorite bad word?'*

Once the game is over, realize you have just shined up this tool in your tool box so the minute the child mumbles a bad word out of frustration, you can whisper, *'Do you want to play the bad word game, again?'* Brilliant - once the permission is given; once the child realizes that this is no longer a parent button to push in order to seek inappropriate attention; there won't be many situations for the child to use bad words. After all, the truth of the matter is the child learned the bad word from the adult/child, the parent. Children watch and listen to everything; even your frustrations and expressions of the moment. Ultimately you may even suggest, since they probably already recognize that 'big' people tend to say bad words-often, that when they are sixteen years old, they too can say bad words. Miracle workers come up with these ideas.

Hmmm, I know you'll have to think about this one. Stick this tool in your tool box, risk using it one day and be amazed. Don't let the tool fall too far to the bottom of the tool box; you may use it sooner than you think!

As for Brother Jimmy, the one who is always yelled at and can't seem to do anything right, he may even be considered the bad one, the one you love to hate, the 'wicked' one in the family. Who is the wicked one in your family? That one particular family member in the pecking order that really is the one the family should be listening to? Like Wicked, the very popular Broadway Musical.

In 1995, author Gregory Maguire forever changed the paradigm on the classic children's story The Wizard of Oz. According to his Broadway Musical, Wicked the good witch is really the bad witch and the bad witch (Elphaba) was always the good witch??? Through the ages, could it be all change agents, all truth sayers and integrity minded family members; the scapegoats were labeled "wicked" for telling the truth?

Is this true even today? Is today's world much different? Could it be true that many of us don't step up and tell the truth because we would be judged, picked on, even ridiculed? Virtually aren't we being called 'wicked' for letting the truth out of the bag, out of the closet? We are looked down upon, frowned upon for speaking up. Of course, we know now this is just noise. The louder the noise, the more it proves we are on the right track. The louder the noise, the more we can make imaginary check marks in the air indicating we were right in thinking that change would come sooner than later, 'They' just aren't ready to *know* ---yet!

Kudos to the courageous and fearless Brother Jimmies, Miss Annies and Elphabas in the world. The miracle workers are making a difference! Won't you join us? Angels know we are overdue-- *"Ahhhh!"*

3DL or 4DL is a choice, which lifestyle do you choose?

Know– *Synonyms–*realize, discern, be positive, be confident, have no doubt, feel certain, be assured, have knowledge, have information, be informed, recognize, perceive, notice, see, be cognizant, be wise

OR

Know– *Antonyms–*be ignorant, or illiterate, overlook, misunderstand, misconstrue, unacquainted, unfamiliar with.

Scene Eighteen

Held Accountable

In this scene an exhausted Miss Annie gives Mom a report on how Helen is capable of manners at the dinner table, IF she is held accountable.

Kate: *What happened?*
Miss Annie: *She ate from her own plate. She ate with a spoon... herself. And she folded her napkin.*
Kate: *Folded-- her napkin?*
Miss Annie: *The room's a wreck, but her napkin is folded. I'll be in my room, Mrs. Keller.*
Viney: *Don't be long, Miss Annie. Dinner'll be ready right away.*
Kate: *Folded her napkin...My Helen folded her napkin?*

Miss Annie finishes sharing with Helen's mom and says she'll be in her room. She was exhausted to be sure. Miss Annie later journals about this breakfast scene:

"I had a good cry and feel better. I suppose I shall have many such battles with the little woman before she learns the only two essential things I can teach her, obedience and love."
Annie Sullivan, The Story of My Life p.256

For the first time in all of Helen's seven years, she has been asked to behave like the rest of the family. Is it too much to ask Helen to eat with a spoon from her own plate, instead of walking around the table grabbing at whatever she wants? What about actually sitting with the family for dinner? Would it be too much to ask if Helen could fold her napkin like the rest of the family? If you think it is, then you are absolutely right, and change will <u>never</u> happen; status quo will prevail in your family. That sounds like settling and giving up to me!

For the first time, Helen was asked to be accountable at the dining table. Imagine being allowed to do as you please everyday of your life and then being told, by a virtual stranger, that you can no longer have things your way, to behave at your whim. Your world has just been turned upside down! The problem is, as the adult, if you let one inappropriate behavior slip by without saying anything, then another inappropriate behavior will slip by, and then another and so on. This usually occurs because the child is confused about what is expected of them, so they continue on a downward spiral never even considering their behavior is suspect. There needs to be guidance, there needs to be direction and discipline, and honestly, they want to know. How many adult/children do you know who are still moving along in life on the downward spiral?

As an adult, you've probably experienced individuals with these types of behavior either at work, with neighbors, or even from a church member. Many times it is difficult to believe adult/children actually behave the way they do. Were they never told or taught about manners and respect? Where were their particular adult role models? *Who* were their adult role models? When will you decide for yourself that it's no longer appropriate to tolerate inappropriate behaviors within your family, or in your business? When will you decide to stand firm about what are acceptable and unacceptable behaviors? It is finally time for accountability.

Today is the day! Are you willing to risk a tug of war similar to the tug of war Miss Annie experienced with Helen at breakfast? Just because Miss Annie decided Helen should be taught how to fold her napkin! So trivial, or is it? Even the smallest request is appropriate and expected when you are trying to instill better behavior, proper manners and character development - all of which are fundamental and basic overall social skills.

—◦◦◦◦◦—

Possible Miracle Worker Dialog: Context Sensitive

A good way to introduce change is coming, start with… *'I have made a mistake that I would like to share with you. I have not made it clear enough about what behaviors would be acceptable and what behaviors would not be. It may feel like I'm on your case, always after you and demanding better. I ask you to do better because I know you <u>can</u> do better. I can do better too! As we both work toward doing better during this journey you won't always like it or me, and I'm ok with that. I love myself enough to say it out loud and I love you enough to make that difference.'* Whether you say all this to an actual individual or not, doesn't matter. What matters is you believe it and begin to live it!

Then there is the time to celebrate! There is always time for celebration. Hope, trust and keep the faith - your miracle is right around the corner. Look around you and perhaps notice someone who may have a smile on their face, or a skip in their walk indicating life is good. *'I can see you are celebrating. What's new and different in your life?'* Acknowledge someone who is celebrating. Celebrating is what we want most in life. If we can acknowledge that celebration moment then the conversation will be centered on positive events instead of negative. Now that is something to truly celebrate!

—◦◦◦◦◦—

Today is the day! Reach in, grab your courage and risk molding your adult/children from the inside out. It may seem like it takes far too much time, and I can promise you that the necessary time you must invest is all part of the initial 'start up' costs. Your adult/child's behavior may in fact worsen initially and your life may prove to be more chaotic in the process. I can also promise that everything will get worse before your adult/children get better. I can also promise you everything will be for the better, and Helen is our greatest example of this.

"The great step-the step that counts-has been taken. The little savage has learned her first lesson; obedience, and finds the yoke easy. It now remains my pleasant task to direct and mould the beautiful intelligence that is beginning to stir in the child-soul."
Annie Sullivan, The Story of My Life p.260

"The little savage" - don't we all feel that way about our children from time to time, let alone an adult/child?

What a Miracle Worker Would Share

Like Helen, your child will try every cunning trick in the book in order to have you respond in the way you used to respond. Cunning children don't want to learn a new dance; they are comfortable with the old tried and true steps. Tantrums will be longer, tantrums will be louder. But don't give up - it will be worth it in the end.

"You see that she is very bright, but you have no idea how cunning she is."
Annie Sullivan, The Story of My Life, p.263.

Children are all very cunning - aren't we all, even the adult/child?

Miss Annie first arrived at Ivy Green, the Keller estate, on March 3rd, 1887, three months before Helen turned 7. It took her a little over two weeks of an intense combination of hard work, insistence and dedication to teach a deaf and blind child to have enough decorum in order to be reached on an internal level. Miss Annie did spend her entire career, life with Helen. Balancing better behavior can last a lifetime, all filled with constant reminders, toying with win/win situations, allowing for consequences, reminding again… Parents, just by their presence, could become the reminder of the integrity any child needs to adopt. Make the effort; model and guide the child. Imagine what young ladies and gentlemen we would have today. Is today the day of change at your house? What a wonderful world this could be.

"And it is not three months yet since she learned her first word. It is a rare privilege to watch the birth, growth, and first feeble struggles of a living mind; this privilege is mine; and moreover, it is given me to rouse and guide this bright intelligence."
Annie Sullivan, The Story of My Life p.272

Imagine being the proud parent of a child and fully understanding the bigger picture of having the rare privilege of watching *"the birth, growth and first feeble struggles of a healthy living mind."* The privilege is yours too; you have been blessed with a beautiful child, and hopefully, like Miss Annie, you've decided to take on the challenge... *"It is given me to rouse and guide this bright intelligence."* Hear the words again... *"a healthy living mind"*... Listen for the Angels: *'Ahhhh!...'*

3DL or 4DL is a choice, which lifestyle do you choose?

Accountable– *Synonyms*–liable, answerable, responsible, obligated, chargeable, culpable, blameworthy

OR

Accountable– *Antonyms*–blameless, exempt, innocent, guiltless, excused.

Scene Nineteen

Miss Annie Reminisces

Several ladies are debating about a blind school and young Annie is very interested. Miss Annie reminisces about the time she learned there could be a school for her.

- *There is a school.*
- *There is not.*
- *What lies are you telling the ignorant girl, you old loon?*
- *They teach blind ones worse than her.*
- *To do what? See with their nose?*
- *To read and write.*
- *How can they read and write if they can't see?*
- *(screaming) You crazy old Mick.*
Jimmy: *You ain't going to school, are you Annie?*
Annie: *When I grow up.*
Jimmy: *You ain't either, Annie. You said we'd be together forever and ever and ever.*
Annie: *I'm going to school when I grow up! Now leave me be.*
- *They are all here. Talk to them.*
- *You can get out. Talk to them.*
- *All the investigators are here.*
- *That's Mr. Sanborn. He's the commissioner. Talk to him. You might get out.*
Annie: *Mr. Sanborn? Mr. Sanborn, I want to go to school.*

Miss Annie reflects back on memories, many of which aren't happy. None the less, her memories draw out solutions to help with the current situation she faces. It forces Miss Annie to go within, to seek answers and solutions. For Miss Annie, what past experiences, uniquely and Divinely orchestrated can she draw from to help her in her current situation?

122

An important point to recognize here is the realization that Miss Annie reaches within; she's connecting her heart with her mind for solutions. She's calling on all of her past life's experiences. She's searching in the archives of her being for answers, her virtual essence, her makeup, everything that is Miss Annie… her Spirit. As if thinking out loud, we see her inner workings busy connecting dots. The special and resonant memory of her school days prompts Miss Annie to think about Dr. Howe and how his work influenced her. This memory then propels her to immediately search for Dr. Howe's book and read a specific section for answers and solutions.

We may not always understand the grand plan the Universe provides to us, but you may notice when you look back that your combined life experiences have led you to this particular point in time. Both good and bad experiences make you the person you are. Combined experience is the essence of who you are… your Spirit.

Miss Annie's several combined life experiences made her the exceptional person she became. She endured an alcoholic father who abused her and a mother who died of tuberculosis when Miss Annie was eight years old. Her parents could no longer take care of her or her brother and they eventually became wards of the state. She was sent to an institution along with her brother who also died of tuberculosis at a very young age. Not necessarily a charmed life, but definitely a combination of magical ingredients that gave Miss Annie the tools to become a very successful educator in spite of her upbringing.

Other important ingredients from her life experiences include Miss Annie almost becoming blind herself, living in the North East, attending the Perkins School, and ultimately working and learning from Dr. Howe. Dr. Howe was that special individual who worked with blind students at the Perkins School. All these magical ingredients gave Miss Annie the necessary tools to become very successful with little Helen.

———————

Possible Miracle Worker Dialog- Context Sensitive

There are so many memories that we experience in a lifetime. Unfortunately we usually remember the memories that aren't so great, especially those that haunt us throughout our lives. What mantra-type phrase can we come up with and share over and over to help minimize the negative memories in our life? How about … *'Create a great day!'*

In the end it is up to us to have the life we want. What would that be? What does that look like? *'Create, create, create a great day everyday!'* Watch your life unfold in all its Divine perfection. With newfound understanding and a warrior-like attitude, what will you create today?

———————

Understanding the bigger picture, all of her life experiences, both happy and the not so happy, brought Miss Annie to the exact time and space for her to be ready, to accept, and to embark upon on her journey of purpose. Here is some interesting background information on Dr. Samuel Gridley Howe, the man who was a strong influence in Miss Annie's life: Divinely orchestrated, of course!

"Dr. Samuel Gridley Howe was born in Boston, November 10, 1801, and died in Boston, January 9, 1876. He was a great philanthropist, interested especially in the education of all defectives, the feeble-minded, the blind and the deaf. Far in advance of his time he advocated many public measures for the relief of the poor and diseased, for which he was laughed at then, but which have since been put into practice. As head of the Perkins Institution for the Blind in Boston, he heard of Laura Bridgman and had her brought to the Institution on October 4, 1837. Laura Bridgman was born at Hanover, New Hampshire, December 12, 1829; so she was almost eight years old when Dr. Howe began experiments with her. At the age of twenty-six months scarlet fever left her without sight or hearing. Dr. Howe was an experimental scientist and had in him the Spirit of New England Transcendentalism with its large faith and large charities. Science and faith led him to try to make his way into the soul which he believed was born in Laura Bridgman as in every other human being"

Story of My Life- p243

What a Miracle Worker Would Share

What past experiences, both good and not so good, can you draw from when working with your children and even adult/children? In spite of how you were raised, can you move past any anger, bitterness and life confusions and reach within for your potential? How often do you stop to take a moment, take a deep breath and focus on the immediate moment? How often do you reach into the depths of who you are; the combined experiences of your makeup -your Spirit- for answers and solutions?

On a symbolic, metaphysical level, your combined life experiences up to this point, as well as future experiences, are all being acquired by you in order to support your life quest, if you want. Hopefully, you will begin to see the value of the various twists and turns life takes for you, all of which makes for better understanding and decision making. Really - take a look at it. What past experiences, good and bad, can you draw from to create your life? What does Mom do that influences your life and makes you want to follow in her footsteps, or maybe you know you don't want to follow in her footsteps? What about Dad? What friend, neighbor or extended family member influenced your life? Consider health issues that prompted you to delve into the field of medicine, chiropractic or a massage career? Is this where you belong? Is this your life's passion? How did you get there? Is this what your Spirit really wants, or does it cry out for something else?

Remember, we all have good and bad experiences. We can make wise choices or not so wise choices according to our life experiences. Choices are exactly that, a choice. Every decision, every direction taken is a choice. Bad choices are not meant to be used as convenient excuses for life going bad; rather change the choice that you typically make. We can make life as easy as we want to, or as difficult as we want. By taking a moment to look at these intricate workings, these life puzzle pieces, we can tap into that well of knowledge and recognition, and see that the Universe is very hard at work. After all, it is this unique combination of Divine life experiences that point you toward your life's purpose. Begin to trust that the Universe has its hand in your growth and development. It is, nevertheless your own choice to choose a Spiritual growth and development - fulfilled lifestyle. Are you ready?

You can immediately and easily assess whether or not life is aligned or not with your heart and mind. If your life seems to be a struggle with nothing working out easily, and you're feeling as if you are always back tracking, then take a moment to listen. If one step forward and two steps back are your life indicators, then you are not in your Spirit. You aren't listening and making wise choices. Luck is not on your side. Begin to notice those moments when life seems lucky. Was it luck or better choices? It may be the road less traveled, but celebrate being different and enjoy the journey of what is to become uniquely yours. I'll bet Miss Annie never dreamed she would move to Tuscumbia, Alabama - the road less traveled!

What will you choose today, 3DL or 4DL? Listen for the Angels, when you choose wisely, or as kids today say, 'Spot On!' you will hear them *"Ahhhh!"*.

3DL or 4DL is a choice, which lifestyle do you choose?

Choice– *Synonyms–*choosing, decision, deciding, discretion, option, voice, determination

OR

Choice– *Antonyms–*coercion, force, command, order, indifferent

Scene Twenty

Dr. Howe's Primer

A frustrated, but determined, Miss Annie searches for Dr. Howe's guide looking for answers and solutions on how to handle little Helen. Flustered, she reads:

"Can nothing be done to disinter this human soul? The whole neighborhood would rush to save this woman if she were buried alive by the caving in of a pit, and labor with zeal until she were dug out. Now, if there were one who had as much patience as zeal, he might awaken her... might awaken her to a consciousness of her immortal nature. The chance is small indeed, but with a smaller chance they would have dug desperately for her in the pit. And is the life of the soul of less import than that of the body?"

Amazing! This represents a truly amazing moment in the Helen Keller story. Simply analyzed, a whole neighborhood would rush to save a woman if she were buried alive with both labor and zeal until she was dug out. *"And is the life of the soul of less import than that of the body?"* In the present moment, would we do less? Would we take the patience, zeal and labor to dig out a child's Spirit? Would we take the time and awaken the child *"to a consciousness of her immortal nature"*?

Can you hear the Angels celebrating? They are dancing with joy. This is an amazing and life-awakening concept. Yet what school today would openly encourage a conversation of this nature? In today's world, would this type of discussion be crossing over some inappropriate line? What is that line exactly? Without reaching an individual's Spirit is there only a life of confusion and chaos? Is this need the missing piece of successfully living the game of life? If we just tap into our individual Spirit's wants

127

and needs, would that make life easier and less dysfunctional? Miss Annie was certainly onto something here. Dr. Howe and Miss Annie felt and understood what we've come to recognize as the 4DL shift, even if they didn't call it 4DL.

A rather chilling statement, to be sure: *"And is the life of the Soul of less import than that of the body?"* Do we have life's priorities a bit backwards being available to save a human life at a moment's notice, but not the Soul? Why not both?

Possible Miracle Worker Dialog- Context Sensitive

Soul - what is a Soul and what does it do? The Soul is simply the living potential of any given individual. Let this become your new quest-- go ahead and dig out an adult/child's Spirit; call them out... *'I love you enough to champion your will, your Soul, your Spirit. If you aren't busy striving and creating potential, you are not in your Spirit. What is missing, what do you need?'*

Consider the current Consciousness Movement underway in today's world. Many Spiritual centers have opened up. There are so many self-help books and tapes to which we can refer. There is a multitude of historical information, and so many old philosophies and beliefs that are being rediscovered, coming to the forefront and now being labeled New Age. What is with all this new interest in the last couple of years? What are people really looking for when they visit and buy these types of books and tapes? Are they looking for their Spirit, are they trying to discover their true nature, their potential? Are they searching for 4DL? Where do we look for information on how to reach anyone's Spirit? Who will call you out on behavioral dramas? Who will be honest enough with you to share the truth that you say you want to hear? Who will be the Miss Annie in your life?

"Now, if there were one who had as much patience as zeal, he might awaken her... might awaken her to a consciousness of her immortal nature. The

chance is small indeed, but with a smaller chance they would have dug desperately for her in the pit. And is the life of the soul of less import than that of the body?"

This is probably the most important quote in the story of <u>The Miracle Worker</u>. Miss Annie's ability to grasp this concept is truly a natural gift. She came into this world imbued with this gift. She understood that the Soul was just as important as the body, which many parents today just don't understand, or don't even consider. They don't even understand themselves and their own Spirit, so realistically how could they possibly understand their child's? If you are not in your Spirit, how is it possible to help your child to discover theirs? How will you reach your Spirit so you can have successful, healthy, productive and independent children? What personal growth and development course will you take? Do you have a Spiritual advisor you consult with to find balance in life? What is your next step, are you even looking? Understand clearly, reaching your Spirit will be the gauge for successful children, for a successful future. The clue is noticing what behaviors they mirror.

For those of us who don't understand the "life of the soul", we have to learn the difference, just like Helen's parents. They will have to learn how to reach Helen on a Spirit level, or else she is prone to fall back into her dysfunctional ways, as we will see. It is that fast and easy to simply resort back to the old 3DL way of acting, of living, rather than continue to focus and grab for 4DL way of life.

In 1887, in a report about Miss Annie, Mr. Anagnos says: *"She was obliged to begin her education at the lowest and most elementary point; but she showed from the very start that she had in herself the force and capacity which insure success. She has finally reached the goal for which she strove so bravely."*

The Story of My Life p 248

What a Miracle Worker Would Share

Recognize how amazing it is to consider allowing a child to live, to be, in their Spirit - to reach full potential, to be the essence of what he/she was meant to be. What a great moment when Miss Annie looks around the room in despair and grabs Dr. Howe's book for some solutions. This small book excerpt allows Miss Annie to consider that the answer could be found in the Soul - the Spirit. It gives Miss Annie the necessary permission and understanding of how she can accomplish nothing to successfully reach Helen, if she doesn't reach Helen's Spirit first. The Angels are celebrating for sure on this one… *"Ahhhh!"*

We don't even allow for this type of discussion in today's world, or more importantly, in today's schools. It seems there is a lot of dodging concerning the issues of Spirit, although all child advocates, teachers, principals, guidance counselors… are ostensibly there to 'reach' children. Interesting too, we spend a lot of time wanting to know more about raising consciousness which leads us to search in places like bookstores, especially metaphysical bookstores. Do we actually realize what we are looking for? I think not. If we did, we would act and be more advanced; much like high school students with many more tools to work with, preparing for college work. Rather, we act like preschoolers, not even recognizing the simplest of tools in front of us.

When will you grab the better tool for yourself and for your child? When will you make the effort to live a 4DL as the first choice in life rather than the 3DL choices? Eventually, and I'll bet sooner rather than later, the consciousness movement, the better life-choices movement, the common sense movement will encourage a strong 4DL belief system. Let today be the day for you. *Angelsss--*

3DL or 4DL is a choice, which lifestyle do you choose?

Spirit– *Synonyms–*full of spirit, lively, frisky, fiery, courageous, plucky, nervy, fearless, bold

OR

Spirit– *Antonyms–*lifeless, dejected, depressed, despondent, down, downcast, downhearted, droopy, indifferent, lifeless, low, subdued, flat, broken

Scene Twenty-One

Fighting Change

Captain Keller does not understand Miss Annie's ways. From his perspective Miss Annie has ruined any chance at all of getting along with Helen, but Miss Annie knows differently and so does Mom. Captain Keller expresses his frustrations to Kate.

Captain Keller: Let alone the question of who's to pay for the broken dishware. From the moment she came, she's been nothing but a burden. Incompetent, impertinent, ineffectual, immodest and...
Kate: She folded her napkin, Cap'n.
Captain Keller: She what?
Kate: Not ineffectual. Helen did fold her napkin.
Captain Keller: What in heaven's name is so extraordinary about foldin' a napkin?
Kate: Well, it's more than you did, Cap'n.
Captain Keller: Kate, the fact is, today she scuttled any chance of gettin' along with the child. If you can see any point or purpose to her staying on here longer, it's more than I can.
Kate: What do you wish me to do?
Captain Keller: I want you to give her notice.
Kate: I can't.
Captain Keller: Then if you won't, I must.

After the breakfast fiasco Captain Keller discusses with Kate his need for Miss Annie to change her behavior, to change her approach. Miss Annie will not hear of it. She knows these skirmishes are carried out on purpose as well thought out steps and are important for the end result, and so does Mrs. Keller. Mom is impressed Helen folded her napkin.

For once Kate has hope. Kate won't be able to give Miss Annie the notice the Captain asks for, so he takes on the task himself.

Success with Helen will help everyone rethink their position about Miss Annie. Little is the success so far, but Kate can already see it. Where in your life have you had to hold onto your convictions for the sake of a desired result? Kate can see the hope and won't be party to helping the Captain dismiss Miss Annie. Hang tough. Those of us who hang tough while we wait for the rest of the world to catch up are the true change agents. We are the ones who make the world a better place by insisting on the change. It is through change that dysfunction can be remedied. Without change you will continue to experience dysfunction.

As part of the entire experience of life we are given free will and choices. Free will and choices point us in the direction our life will take. We bounce around in our heads all the different choices and options available to us before we ever take an action. Do we, don't we? Should I, shouldn't I? There are right choices and not so right choices. Depending on how we think, what we are attached to, and what kind of result we hope in life will all combine together and determine what choices we will make. A 3DL choice or a 4DL choice?

Miss Annie had to decide which direction she would go. Which direction will *we* go? Which road will we take as we come upon forked roads? Will we pick the turn to the left or the turn to the right? We have all experienced life going well and life not going so well. When life isn't going so well, it would mean taking a wrong turn. Life going better would be a right turn, a correct turn going in the right direction. The road is smooth and there aren't as many bumps in the road, which would indicate more right or correct turns.

What a great way to gauge whether or not we are heading in the right best direction. Listen carefully for the clues to either turn to the right or to turn to the left. Miss Annie's compass worked, she seemed to have the right direction in mind when working with Helen. Life won't be right until we chose - right. Are you on your path, living a healthy lifestyle, living life on purpose, or are you falling off the path, suffering and experiencing the natural consequences due to wrong choices?

When we take a wrong turn and life is not right, we could consciously connect and realize we need to turn back, making for a better and happier right decision. Now life is one to celebrate.

What a Miracle Worker Would Share

Simply stated, Miss Annie stays focused and isn't bothered by the Kellers attitude about her, especially the very authoritative Captain. The truth is it's none of Miss Annie's business how they receive her and her methods. Will she be less authentic and co-dependent or will she reach within and genuinely approach Helen? The Keller family, on the other hand, has to decide if it's a good thing or not to have Miss Annie as Helen's teacher. Captain Keller isn't quite sure. For the 3DL believer, Captain Keller, so far it's not very promising. For someone tip-toeing into a 4DL belief, Kate, Miss Annie is positioning herself for Helen's success. The parents need to get out of the way!

—⁓•⊶⊷⊶•⁓—

Possible Miracle Worker Dialog: Context Sensitive

There are times when we need to preface our next step. Pre-face the moment. Take a minute to pre-face the situation to think about what obstacles are in the way. From this vantage point you will know what to do and know you will do it. From this vantage place know you will know what to say and prepare to say it. Remain calm, easy to do since you know the direction to take. Trust the right words will come. Validate the current perspective, whether you agree with it or not. Be prepared to speak as if you are wearing their (the recipient's) shoes. We have all been in a position where someone has shared a different perspective. Not always easy to hear. Approach the topic by coming first from a place of understanding this different perspective, as you push through the current confusion. Take on the attitude that you don't want to leave the conversation until there is some mutual understanding between the parties.

'I can understand how this may all seem foreign to you. I ask at this time that you allow me the space to do my work as unconventional, even backwards, as it may seem to you. Please take a step back and trust me. Give me the time

necessary to move forward, even if it feels like we are not moving at all. I am confident with this process and I will be happy to explain and teach it to you.'

——————————————

More often than not, a behavioral situation gets worse before it gets better when a change agent encourages change. This makes perfect sense, as you introduce and encourage the use of new tools instead of old, haggard useless tools. For the individuals using the new tools, it may feel very awkward at first, but once they get the hang of the new tool they will wish they knew about it long ago. Now you have won them over - forever. Hang tough and readjust when you need to. Go within, find your own Spirit and listen for Divine wisdom and ideas, hold on to your Divine wisdom and ideas, honor your Spirit and fearlessly live life on purpose. Hello Angels, *"Ahhhh!"*

3DL or 4DL is a choice, which lifestyle do you choose?

Purpose– *Synonyms*–on purpose, deliberately, intentionally, consciously, with intent, calculatedly, expressly, willfully, by design, knowingly,

OR

Purpose– *Antonyms*–accidentally, unintentionally, inadvertently, unknowingly, unconsciously, unthinkingly, by chance

Scene Twenty-Two

Asking for Change

How ironic - in this scene Captain Keller asks Miss Annie for behavior change!

Captain Keller: *Miss Sullivan?*
Miss Annie: *Captain Keller, I thought we should-- have a talk.*
Captain Keller: *Yes, I... Well, come in. Miss Sullivan, I have decided...I have decided I'm not satisfied. In fact, I'm deeply dissatisfied.*
Miss Annie: *Excuse me. Is that little house near the bridge used?*
Captain Keller: *In the huntin' season.*
Miss Annie: *Mrs. Keller I...*
Captain Keller: *If you'll give me your attention, Miss Sullivan I've made allowances because you come from a part of the country where people are women, I should say—come from who— (clears throat) or whom allowances must be made. I have decided nevertheless to... Miss Sullivan, I find it difficult to talk through those glasses. Why do you wear them? The sun's been down for an hour.*
Miss Annie: *Any kind of light hurts my eyes.*
Captain Keller: *Put them on, Miss Sullivan. I've decided... to give you another chance.*
Miss Annie: *To do what?*
Captain Keller: *To remain in our employ. But on two conditions. I'm not accustomed to rudeness. If you are to stay, there must be a radical change of manner.*
Miss Annie: *Whose?*
Captain Keller: *Yours, young lady! Isn't it obvious? And you must persuade me there's the slightest hope of your teaching a child who flees from you like the plague to anyone in this house.*

How cute is this? Captain Keller thinks Miss Annie is a problem and asks her for character change if she is to remain in their employment. Miss Annie on the other hand, is thinking Helen's parents need character change. Miss Annie doesn't know what the Captain is talking about, nor does she consider his perspective. She's too focused on a new idea of what's next for Helen. She has Helen's best interest in mind.

Many times when a 3DL slip-up is apparent, it is easier to blame others for the mishap or misfortune. For Captain Keller it is easier to blame the new girl. It is very difficult and very rare to actually look at the self as part of the problem. Anything or anyone who gets in the way of life for the good of the life lesson is most likely in the way of the growth trying to reveal itself. No one ever wants to consider the life problems around them are the direct result of their own particular behavior; pointing fingers and blaming others is so much easier. What a great way to stay in denial. What a great way to avoid what needs to be dealt with. What a great way to avoid overcoming the life lesson.

In today's world with all the wonderful resources available, other family members may be encouraged to attend some sort of support group or therapy session in order to realize the role that they've played in the family dynamics, and to learn how they arrived at where they are. In reality, everyone plays a role in a family's dysfunction. Two key participant roles are the enablers and the co-depenÂers. Certainly everyone in Helen's home has enabled her. How could you not with a child who can't see or hear? The enablers have a soft spot in their heart, they want to pity, and they always want to help out. Although they mean well, they are active participants to a fault. Truth is, if they stay busy 'helping' others then they don't have to look or deal with their own life; they are too busy muddling in someone else's life. They can avoid creating their own life, they look good and they call it 'helping'. How would anyone find fault or judge them - after all, they are 'helping'!

The clue here is to recognize the act of staying 'busy' to a fault. When we are so busy helping and supporting others, we can't help or support ourselves. Essentially we are in <u>their</u> Spirit. If we are in their Spirit, we can't be in our own. We will never accomplish what we are here to accomplish - our own pure potential.

The co-dependers in the family usually know that something has to be done differently but don't take any action to make the necessary changes. They settle and take on the behavior belief of 'peace at all cost.' They wouldn't want to rock the boat and possibly make matters worse, so they take a back seat and don't take any action at all. They virtually walk on egg shells, not wanting to cause a fuss. They may indeed have an idea, a solution to help solve problems, but they don't risk saying what needs to be said for fear of saying the wrong thing and offending those involved. If we were to take this a step further and go a little deeper we could readily admit - we don't say what needs to be said because we are afraid of how it will be accepted. We fear the reprisal, we fear the rejection.

What a Miracle Worker Would Share

In this scene I'm referring to the Keller family behaviors as 'cute'. All behavior is 'cute'. This is, of course, a play on the word - cute. If we can observe our good behaviors and our not so good behaviors as simply cute and recognize we are in the depths of our life lesson - roaming from 3DL to 4DL - then we can see and accept the behavior as cute. We don't then have to beat ourselves up or even think we need years of therapy. Rather, we are right where we need to be to overcome all the obstacles and grow toward our personal life lessons. Those Angels are dancing and singing now, *"Ahhhh!"*

In this scene, what's also cute is that the Keller family just doesn't get it. They think Helen fleeing from Miss Annie is the real problem, without realizing the family has just embarked upon a new adventure which will turn all their lives around - for the better. This will take time and not much change can be realized, especially if the family continues to resist. With change comes the reality that things will no doubt get worse before anything can get better. After all, if you want to make someone mad, ask them to change!

Let's remember, the reason for the Kellers bringing Miss Annie to work with Helen. It would require the change agent, Miss Annie, to be the change she wishes to see. This may be quite contrary to what the Kellers are used to, or what they expect to happen. That is a good thing, to be contrary, to be an opposite, to be different. It's not important and it shouldn't be expected that the method will be the same. In this case with Helen, it's very important to be different. If Miss Annie came to the Keller family and did just as the Kellers did, then nothing would change; there would be no need for a change agent. Who then would deal with Helen? The family would continue to experience the insanity of repeating over and over what has always been done. Fortunately, at least in the Keller family since we know the end of the story, there will be a time when being different will in fact be welcomed and celebrated.

We can all become change agents, saying those hard to say things. Imagine if each of us once a week championed the will of the one we love. Imagine each week sharing our beliefs and observations because we cared more about the loved one than we did about the reprisal. And, what if once a week turned into twice a week? Eventually, as the recipient, we would come to learn to accept the wisdom of the comment instead of fear it. We could actually lean into the conversation wide-eyed asking for more information since *'I don't see it from your perspective, tell me more.'* Now that would be pure consciousness, wanting to know instead of just saying 'No' to the gift of consciously connecting to something you've never previously considered.

Possible Miracle Worker Dialog--Context Sensitive

Consider a bewildered, frazzled friend coming to you asking for advice. Take a moment to begin with a statement such as, *'I want to hear everything you have to tell me, then I will be happy to share my thoughts.'* Or *'I've been noticing something I would like to share although it may seem critical, would you like to hear it?'* Respectfully, in any relationship even a child to adult relationship; it is important to ask for permission, give a heads up before you share. At the appropriate time continue with, *'I've heard what you said, you may not like what I have to share.'* Wait for the recognition reflex or the verbal permission to share your thoughts. If there is no permission, walk away-gently, calmly and know the Universe will provide another opportunity when they are willing to consider a different perspective.

For those individuals who go on in their description of helplessness and hopelessness, so stuck in their misguided beliefs, be prepared to pre-face. Many times we run into the same conversation from the same individual, again! You may even notice you are nodding your head and not necessarily because you agree, although that is exactly what they would like from you. The nodding of the head could mean… *'Yep, I need to say something. I'm not serving them by allowing them to continue to believe they have right thinking.'* Of course this may mean risking anger and reprisal, but you are up to the task because you love them enough to do so. Easing your way into a shift, you could begin with *'Oh, so you don't know.'* OR *'No-one told you?'* How you say these statements is critical to encouraging an open and honest dialog. If the body language tells you they don't want to hear it, gently and calmly leave and know the Universe will provide another opportunity. The Universe will always provide another opportunity for situations that are not healed.

—~~·o&+o&+o·~~—

For all the change agents and Miss Annies out there trying to make a difference, or at least not giving up on the changes they know are necessary in order to overcome life challenges/opportunities - in defense of your courage and fearlessness to directly deal with the issues, *know* the Angels honor and support you. Hear them- *"Ahhhh!"* Well worth repeating … *'In defense of your courage and fearlessness to directly deal with the issues, know the Angels honor and support you.'*

3DL or 4DL is a choice, which lifestyle do you choose?

Deal– *Synonyms–*treat, handle, oversee, attend to, see to, take care of, cope with, dispose of

OR

Deal– *Antonyms–*ignore overlook, disregard, neglect, leave undone

Scene Twenty-Three

Hope

Captain Keller continues to think the problem is Miss Annie. Mom knows differently.

Captain Keller: Yours, young lady! Isn't it obvious? And you must persuade me there's the slightest hope of your teaching a child who flees from you like the plague to anyone in this house.
Miss Annie: There isn't.
Kate: What, Miss Annie?
Miss Annie: It's hopeless here.
Captain Keller: Then-- do I understand—you propose...
Miss Annie: Well, if we agree it's hopeless, the next question is--
Kate: Miss Annie, I'm not agreed. She did fold her napkin. She learns. She learns. Do you know she began talking when she was six months old? She could say water. Well, not really. Wah-wah. Wah-wah. But she meant water. She knew what it meant, and only six months old. I never saw a child so bright or outgoing. It's still in there somewhere, isn't it? Miss Annie, put up with her and with us.

Captain Keller is convinced that there is no hope for Miss Annie. Kate, on the other hand, believes there is hope for Helen. Kate knows Helen is smart, clever, even as early as a six month old. She begs Miss Annie to *"...put up with her and with us."* Mom seems to have a better handle on the situation. Mom is willing to push through the chaos and discover the miracles while waiting patiently for the chaos to be experienced and worked through.

When Miss Annie first arrives at the Keller Estate, Ivy Green, Captain Keller instantly red flags her and her personality. Captain Keller is already doubtful and doesn't trust this 'newcomer'. According to the Captain he has already judged Miss Annie: she's too young, wears funny glasses, he discovers she was blind once herself and has never before held a job position. Worse, she comes from the wrong part of the World! You have to admit, these aren't great qualifications. Remember Scene Six:

Captain Keller: Katie… Sh. She's very rough.
Kate: I like her, Cap'n.
Captain Keller: How old is she?
Kate: Well, she's not in her teens, you know.
Captain Keller: Why does she wear those glasses? I like to see a person's eyes when I talk to 'em.
Kate: For the sun. She was blind.
Captain Keller: Blind?
Kate: She had nine operations on her eyes. One just before she left.
Captain Keller: Blind? Good heavens! They expect one blind child to teach another? How long did she teach there?
Kate: She was a pupil. This is her first position? She was valedictorian.

A new challenge/opportunity has been invited into the Keller home. Trusting is a hard concept to accept. Accepting a new individual who will be living in the house is also very different. Change is difficult too. Certainly the background check on Miss Annie is suspect and an adjustment is required of everyone.

But wait - what a wonderful world we live in! Opportunities are around every corner. In every nook and cranny of our lives there are new activities and special events for the mind, the body and the Spirit. If we are open and aware, we become blessed with an abundance of unique circumstances all waiting to enhance our everyday life. These unique opportunities and circumstances can be helped along and manifested through our positive thoughts, energy and affirmations. Before long we begin to trust in those special occasions when they arrive in life. We trust ourselves and those trustworthy around us. There are less and less obstacles in the way as we move forward, making better choices which manifest into better outcomes. We know the Universe is hard at work, in our honor.

When circumstances and situations go our way, some would call that luck, but we know luck isn't what it's all about. Luck plays such a minor role in the bigger picture. As individuals, we undertake a very important and active role in creating our life. In losing track of the goal, the dream, and the hope - we lose the luck. Or do we lose the positive thoughts, energy and affirmations that would pro-actively propel us forward and toward our potential and purpose?

If this is the truth and should we lose the positive thoughts, energy, and affirmations, then what are we withholding? Why do we refrain and withdraw from the positive spirals in our life and turn to the negative tornado-like spirals? By the mere act of withholding there is a knowing, a clue that we are 'holding out' and willing to settle. We know exactly what to do yet we refuse to do it. All it took was a brief second to shift and refuse to do it. What a great way to stay stuck, lost, confused; 3DL.

Be aware to such thoughts as, *'I won't give you what you want or need to have.'* Keeping and hoarding information to ourselves; *'I won't tell you what you need to know.'* Check in and see whom it is you might be defiantly holding back from. Could it be with a parent, a business partner, or a personal relationship? Maybe it's not something outside of you, but something within you. You know those hard to look at phrases such as:

- 'I don't deserve to have or to ask for what I want.'
- 'I don't deserve to be happy.'
- 'I don't trust others, I don't trust myself.'

Once we become tired and overwhelmed by these negative outcomes, the pendulum will eventually begin to swing back to positive thoughts, energy and manifestations. Then, we are once again living within a place of trusting, positive outcomes. We must ultimately give ourselves the permission to live authentically. You know - carpe diem!

What a Miracle Worker Would Share

In this scene we recognize Kate sees something special in Miss Annie and likes her. Even if it's just a little hope - a folded napkin, Kate's hanging on. There are times when intuition, gut instinct and trust go a long way. Miss Annie seemed to be spot on with her instinct of how to work with Helen. In this scene there is no mention of the word intuition or trust, but it would be a fine time to consider if using intuition, gut instinct and trust could benefit you and your family.

Possible Miracle Worker Dialog- Context Sensitive

Hope, there is always hope. Hold on to it, embrace possibilities as Hope whispers-- 'try one more time'. Encourage a loved one to *'Think of new ideas, consider different options and explore like pioneers and explorers for new adventures. Lean toward what feels better, what resonates with chills and thrills.'*

Sometimes it's difficult to let go of a child, who may very well need some breathing room, to experience their life lesson without the need of being rescued by a family member. Letting go may be a new idea to consider. It could be time for the child to grow up; time to be age and stage appropriate. It could very well be time for mom or dad to grow up and be age and stage appropriate too. Make room for life experiences to play themselves out. Reach within and grab onto patience and tolerance. Allow the room for drama to play out, trusting that hurdles will be jumped and lessons will be learned. Take off the brakes so the child will develop the strength and courage necessary to handle everyday life challenges, as well as the many new life adventures and experiences to come. You may not understand the whys, and truthfully, the whys aren't important. Lessons are coming either way.

What is important is to trust that the Universe is Divinely orchestrating your family's successes and the bigger ride you are all on, called conscious living. At some point we all decided to experience and participate in this adventure called life. Sometimes it's wonderful. We can feel, touch, love, eat and experience life thrills. Other times life isn't so wonderful, it's darn right difficult - sometimes it just sucks. Overall, we've decided the ride was more important than the bumps and bruises we could get along the way. If we really wrap ourselves around enjoying these worthwhile rides, then we can allow more room for the deeper Spiritual growth and development of friends, families, neighbors and the entire life experience. Enjoy the bumps.

Of course, this doesn't mean we ignore protecting our loved ones and allow for dangerous situations which could harm an individual, especially a child. For children, all situations and circumstances need adult supervision and reality checks. If there is a situation where life, limb or property of another is in jeopardy, by all means use common sense and take care of the problem. Call the proper authorities. There is no excuse, ever, for allowing a child to be harmed. If in doubt check it out, immediately! If you think "it", it's probably true – it is your intuition talking to you. Take action…yesterday!

Are you ready for change? Do you need change in your life? How long can you continue to fool your heart? Life is ours to create, or not to create the dreams, hopes and aspirations we have. The mere act of withholding, of standing back in defiance is the 3DL clue. Results which create fulfilled lifestyles, balance and happiness is the 4DL clue. How do you choose to live?

3DL or 4DL is a choice, which lifestyle do you choose?

Decide– *Synonyms–*determine, resolve, settle, choose, elect, select, make up one's mind.

OR

Decide– *Antonyms–*vacillate, waver, hesitate, falter, fluctuate

Scene Twenty-Four

The Problem Is the Parents

Miss Annie indicates to Mr. and Mrs. Keller she cannot successfully teach Helen… at the house.

Kate: *Miss Annie, I'm not agreed. She did fold her napkin. She learns. She learns. Do you know she began talking when she was six months old? She could say water. Well, not really. Wah-wah. Wah-wah. But she meant water. She knew what it meant, and at only six months old. I never saw a child so bright or outgoing. It's still in there somewhere, isn't it? Miss Annie, put up with her and with us.*
Captain Keller: *Us?*
Kate: *Please. Like the lost lamb in the parable, I love her all the more.*
Miss Annie: *Mrs. Keller, I don't think Helen's worst handicap is deafness or blindness. All of you here are so sorry for her; you've kept her- like a pet. Why, even a dog you house-break. It's useless for me to try to teach her language or anything else here.*

Strong language; it reaches right to the core. Captain Keller is at a total loss; he is clueless. Miss Annie's comments about the role the Kellers have played in Helen's life may be the very first time the Captain has ever heard such a shocking truth. Has anyone ever dared approach, especially the Captain, on the issue that Helen's worst handicap may not even be about her physical handicaps? What an eye opener for the Kellers, to be accused of feeling *"sorry"* for Helen. Even more shocking is the comparison Miss Annie chose so that her point would hit home: *"All of you here are so sorry for her; you've kept her like a pet. Why, even a dog you housebreak."*

Miss Annie is the one to ultimately break the news that it's the parents that are in need of a character change. How can a change agent like Miss Annie effectively implement change if she can't be honest and 'break the news'? I'm sure Helen's parents never considered the depth of the problem; they do indeed play a huge role in the problem. I'm sure many parents today never consider the depth of their position within their family problem. This is unfortunate but at the same time very much the reality of parents who remain in denial. The truth is, the children see, watch and hear everything going on in the home. They adopt the attitudes, energy, rituals and beliefs of everyone they are first exposed to, and that would obviously be the parents, the child's first teacher.

Do not underestimate what the child learns at the hands of the parents, within the home. For example, just look in the mirror - if you are a confident and self-reliant individual, the child will be confident and self-reliant. If you are not confident then the child will also develop less confidence. What does your child need from you? Could it possibly be true that the best way to bring up a child is to be a self-assured, responsible, accountable, successful, independent, capable, creative parent? The truth is-- *If I want to see these qualities in my child, I must possess these qualities myself.* Now there's a concept... it's all in the mirror.

What a Miracle Worker Would Share

Consider family or friends you know who surround themselves with individuals who would pity them, all their lives. Who do you know who loves to be pitied? Who do you know who loves to be a victim? You certainly can generate a lot of inappropriate attention by seeking pity, being needy. When a child is surrounded by loved ones who pity them, the child learns to expect that kind of attention. The attitude the child picks up is, *'See, even they feel sorry for me.'* How do you ever turn that around?

Raise your personal standard. What training, or self esteem skills will you need to raise a confident child? Raise the level of expectation. What is the expectation? What do you expect from your child? How could you expect these qualities in your child if you do not possess them yourself? Teach them, teach them well.

⎯ ⧫⦿⧫⦿⧫ ⎯

Possible Miracle Worker Dialog-Context Sensitive

Consider the appropriate context for these valuable pointed statements. *'What do you need?', 'What do you want?', 'I want what you want.'* After some brainstorming ask *'How will you accomplish that?'* Now negotiate for a win/win. *'I want you to win and I want to win too, let's choose some ideas so we can both win?'*

⎯ ⧫⦿⧫⦿⧫ ⎯

Some adult/children let *reality* become their reality, that is, whatever is, is all they expect out of life. These adult/children let circumstances influence their day as if they have no recourse but to accept them. If being a victim is their reality, then this is what they expect. This would be living a 3DL. Other adult/children let *expectation* be their reality. These individuals are busy creating their day; creating is their reality. Every day they create and expect their reality to proceed in a certain way, in a certain direction which has been very well planned and thought out. They drive the bus, so to speak. They are proactive rather than reactive to their own life circumstances and situations. These adult/children choose a 4DL. This is a choice.

Easier said than done… notice the difference in the following two phrases:

"Have a great day."

OR

"Create a great day."

Which one gives you the 4DL Angel chill? *'Ahhhh!'*

3DL or 4DL is a choice, which lifestyle do you choose?

Expectation– *Synonyms–*look forward to, plan on, look for, envision, anticipate, count on, hope for, believe, surmise, imagine, calculate, contemplate

OR

Expectation– *Antonyms–*despair of, lose faith, dread, fear

Scene Twenty-Five

Creating Autonomy

Miss Annie has a problem, and she also has a solution for the problem. Will Helen's parents agree?

Kate: *Miss Annie, before you came we spoke of putting her in an asylum.*
Miss Annie: *What kind of asylum? For mental defectives. I visited there. I can't tell you what I saw. People like-- animals, with-- rats in the halls and--*
Kate: *What else are we to do if you give up?*
Miss Annie: *Give up?*
Kate: *You said it was hopeless.*
Miss Annie: *Here. Give up? Why, I only today saw what has to be done to begin. I-- want complete charge of her.*
Captain Keller: *You already have that. It has resulted in--*
Miss Annie: *No. I mean day and night. She has to be dependent on me.*
Kate: *For what?*
Miss Annie: *Everything. The food she eats, the clothes she wears, fresh-- air. Yes, the air she breathes. Whatever her body needs is a—primer, to teach her out of. It's the only way, the one who lets her have it should be her teacher-- not anyone who loves her.*
Captain Keller: *But if she runs from you-- to us--.*
Miss Annie: *Yes. That's the point. I'll have to live with her somewhere else.*
Kate: *For how long?*
Miss Annie: *Until she learns to depend and listen to me. I packed half my things all ready.*
Captain Keller: *Miss Sullivan!*
Miss Annie: *Captain Keller it meets both your conditions. It's the one way I can get back in touch with Helen and I don't see how I can't be rude to you again if you're not around to interfere with me.*

Miss Annie has no intention of changing her way or her character. She needs to save every ounce of energy she can muster up for Helen. *"And I can't be rude to you if you're not around."* Miss Annie's comment may even be setting Captain Keller up for the future. She may have to be direct with the Captain many more times in the future… for Helen's good. Unfortunately at this point in time there weren't any Al-Anon programs or Betty Ford Foundations where family members could learn new tools on how to better handle a special needs child like Helen. It could be that Miss Annie just had to be louder and very direct in order to be heard.

Possible Miracle Worker Dialog—Context Sensitive

It is often said of individuals who are struggling in life, and making poor choices that *'They did the best they could.'* This statement is a cop out; the correct statement is *'No, they didn't want to know.'* This is the better statement, the truth of what is going on. Because they didn't want to know and hoped upon hope the situation would take care of itself -- in time, or just go away. Instead of this avoidance approach, find instead the right timing to approach situations head on, and then take the action necessary. Anything else is neglect, and quite simply a fear of conflict. There are too many resources available to find the correct solutions. Affirm… *'Today, I want to know.'*

How clever Miss Annie is to recognize she needs Helen to be dependent only on her, since the parents are in the way. Miss Annie understands Helen could only be effectively reached by being totally dependent on her. Miss Annie has developed a great strategy, to remove Helen from the home environment, away from the family dysfunction. In today's version of an intervention, individuals are often removed from the home and rehabilitated away from the dysfunctions of family life. Miss Annie is encouraging a similar idea. In essence, Miss Annie's idea is to rehab in the old little family cottage, to foster autonomy.

"I mean day and night, for everything. The food she eats, the clothes she wears, fresh… air. Yes, the air she breathes. Whatever her body needs is a primer to teach her out of. The one who lets her have it should be her teacher, not anyone who loves her."

Ironically, Miss Annie isn't even a parent. Miss Annie has no children of her own, and here she is 'driving the bus' in the Keller household. Miss Annie knows the direction to go; she especially knows which direction *not* to go. Where do you acquire this kind of training? Is this a matter of training or is it a matter of bothering to reach inside into the arsenal of tools, wisdom and know-how we all naturally possess? All we have to do is bother.

What a Miracle Worker Would Share

Not for a single minute did Miss Annie consider she was the problem for the recent chaos in the Keller household, even though all fingers were pointed at her. Where's the mirror on this one? Miss Annie caused chaos and, like a mirror, she got chaos, right? Let's look at that. Is Miss Annie's chaos all tied up in ego, superiority and narcissism? Or is Miss Annie's chaos all tied up in right thinking and toward the better thing to do? One of these two statements is 3DL thinking and one is 4DL.

Are you the problem in your home? What life activities did you allow your child to escape from so they wouldn't feel uncomfortable or challenged for their own good? How did you enable? How will you push them back into the game of life in order to master how to get along?

What change agent or miracle worker has been loud, maybe even crass and direct in their approach in order for you to hear? Maybe this person is a family member, close friend or a teacher, or maybe the school principal? Is Miss Annie the change agent for the Kellers? Is she in her ego and needs to be right, or is she trying to turn the belief systems (BS's) of the family around? Who in your life is trying to turn your BS's around? What shocking statement had to be said in order for you to 'hear'? Did you dismiss the statement along with the individual who talked to you so 'rudely'? Was this individual in their ego, or were they truthfully and honestly being direct for the sole purpose of trying to help you, to enlighten you in order to evolve? Angels never tire of you learning… *"Ahhhh!"*

3DL or 4DL is a choice, which lifestyle do you choose?

Direct– *Synonyms*–straightforward, frank, candid, clear, explicit, plain-spoken, point-blank, going straight to the point, sincere, honest, pointed, forward, forthright, blunt

OR

Direct– *Antonyms*–indirect, meandering, roundabout, devious, subtle, sly, oblique

Scene Twenty-Six

There's Always A Solution

Together with Miss Annie, the Keller family brainstorms a solution to find the best way to reach Helen.

Captain Keller: What is your intention if I say no? Pack the other half, for home, and abandon your charge to – to—
Miss Annie: The asylum? I grew up in such an asylum. The State Almshouse. Rats-- my brother Jimmy and I used to play with the rats because we didn't have toys. Maybe you'd like to know what Helen will find there, not on visiting days. One ward was full of the –old women, crippled, blind, most of them dying, but even if what they had was catching there was nowhere to put them, and that's where they put us. There were younger ones across the hall, prostitutes mostly, with T.B. and epileptic fits, and a couple of the kind who-- keep after other girls, especially young ones and some insane. Some just had the DT's. The youngest were in another ward to have babies they didn't want, they started at thirteen, fourteen. They'd leave afterwards, but we played with them too, though a lot of them had sores all over from diseases you're not supposed to talk about, but not many of them lived. Jimmy and I played in the dead-house where they kept the bodies till they could dig--
Kate: Oh, my dear--
Miss Annie: --the graves. No. It made me strong. But I don't think you need send Helen there. She's strong enough.
Kate: Miss Annie.
Miss Annie: Yes?
Kate: Where would you-- take Helen?
Miss Annie: Oh--... Italy.
Captain Keller: What?

Miss Annie: *You can't have everything. How would your little cottage do? Furnish it, bring Helen there after a long ride so she won't recognize it, and you can see her every day. If she doesn't know. Well?*
Kate: *Is that all?*
Miss Annie: *That's all.*
Kate: *Why, Cap'n, with your permission?*
Miss Annie: *If that boy Percy could sleep there, run errands--*
Kate: *We can let Percy sleep there, I think… Captain?*
Miss Annie: *And move in some old furniture.*
Kate: *Captain, do you think that old bed-stead in the barn would do--?*
Captain Keller: *I've not yet consented to Percy! Or the house! Or to the proposal! Or to Miss Sullivan's -- staying on-- when I-- Very well, I consent to everything-- for two weeks. I'll give you two weeks in that place, and it will be a miracle if you can get the child to tolerate you.*
Kate: *Two weeks? Miss Annie, can you accomplish anything in two weeks?*
Captain Keller: *Anything or not, two weeks, then the child comes back to us. Make up your mind, Miss Sullivan, yes or no?*
Miss Annie: *Two weeks? I'll get her to tolerate me.*

Miss Annie is as clever as she can be to facilitate the choice of the little cottage. Miss Annie tries wholeheartedly to negotiate this unconventional change of relocating into the little cottage to Helen's parents. I'm sure agreeing to two weeks is better than nothing, although a little bit tongue and cheek to Miss Annie. Two weeks… imagine for just a moment what that really meant to Miss Annie - an impossible task, daunting, overwhelming? Regardless, Miss Annie is going for it. Call her young and dumb, or incredibly smart and very creative. Either way Miss Annie is up to the task. Anything it takes to get Helen away from the dysfunction/love of the family. There isn't much further hope of success if Miss Annie stays in the Keller household. Miss Annie would have a non-stop struggle with the parents. She would have to explain over and over why she's using this strategy or that strategy, and the importance of it. The parents don't get it. Their pity for Helen is really what's in Miss Annie's way.

"Thus it is, we study, plan and prepare ourselves for a task, and when the hour for action arrives, we find that the system we have followed with such labor and pride does not fit the occasion; and then there's nothing for us to do but rely on something within us, some innate capacity for knowing and doing, which we did not know we possessed until the hour of our great need brought it to light."
Annie Sullivan, The Story of My Life p257

———————

Possible Miracle Worker Dialog—Context Sensitive

Brilliant really! Consider the daily needs of an individual as a primer to teach from. Every day, every moment of every event is an opportunity, a primer with which to use life examples as the training ground. Be prepared to take advantage of these moments.

Posing a simple question is a great way to halt the motion of misguided behavior. To consciously connect with what behavior is really going on. Is the behavior what you really want? If not, consider…

- *'Can I ask a question?'*
- *'Whoa, what's going on here?'*
- *'Do you like that?'*
- *'Is that ok with you?'*

———————

As was mentioned in the last Scene, Miss Annie's suggesting the move to the little cottage is a very similar strategy to today's version of an intervention. The addict has to be removed from the family environment, where the dysfunction flourishes. Addict is such a strong word. Is there an addict in your house? Who is an addict that you know? Is Helen an addict?

Webster's dictionary defines addict as- "To devote or give habitually or compulsively."

Addict- *synonyms* of an addict are:

A) user, junkie, freak, dope fiend as in one addicted to drugs, alcohol, prescription drugs
B) devotee, fan, hound, buff as in one addicted to concerts, music, opera
C) give habitually, yield obsessively, surrender, indulge in, submit as is one addicted to food, sweets, co-dependency, enablers, anorexia, bulimia, shoppers, liars…

Addict- *antonyms* of an addict are:
Withdraw, break the habit, kick the habit, renounce, give up.

So, "Is Helen an addict?" Yes, and so are her family members. All members of the family need to re- evaluate their position and consider how they contribute to the problem. Of course, rehab for the entire family wasn't an option. Regardless, Miss Annie hasn't given up hope; on the contrary, she's just begun. Through sheer common sense and will Miss Annie has been able to do what she feels is best for her charge, Helen. Helen is her job; Helen is the reason why she moved to the South. Miss Annie only has to answer to her one charge. As the professional hired by the Kellers, Miss Annie is recommending that she remove Helen from the home environment. Removing Helen from the home environment removes all distractions; all noise. Now Miss Annie can get down to business.

What a Miracle Worker Would Share

As a young woman, Miss Annie acts very professional and very creative in her thinking, even if she doesn't have much experience. She had to dig down into her Spirit for some intuitive answers on what she could do to help herself, thus helping Helen. With a bit of negotiating Miss Annie was able to get the Kellers to agree to a move into the little cottage. What do you need to maneuver and/or negotiate? What could you create that would make a difference to help yourself?

"If only I were better fitted for the great task? I feel every day more and more inadequate.
My mind is full of ideas; but I cannot get them into working shape. You see, my mind is undisciplined, full of skips and jumps, and there are a lot

of things huddled together in dark corners. How I long to put it in order!
Oh, if only there were someone to help me!
I need a teacher quite as much as Helen."
Annie Sullivan, Story of My Life, p.272

How vulnerable! Miss Annie has her doubts. She feels unfit for the job, confused and overwhelmed. Many times we have our own doubts, feel unfit, confused and overwhelmed especially in a new work environment. Family matters become clouded, we become clouded, slink back and blend in with the clouds. We could float along with the clouds and pretend the problems and issues don't exist. Or we could push through the haze and do the right thing. What could we create and strive for as we resolve problems?

Of course there is something to be said for youth. The amount of energy, dedication and patience has not yet been snuffed out by the supposed elders who know better. The youth aren't burnt out from having to constantly pick themselves up and dust themselves off to try again. How great to be young and in a sense, dumb. Like a bull in a china shop, big and bulky as they push through, breaking whatever is in their path. They may not be very gentle in their approach or in their style, but they continue on. They carry on with each step that they take. The young are created for adventure, to endure, like the original pioneers crossing the prairie. They trek on till they get to their final destination, defying all obstacles. Take Miss Annie's lead and if nothing else, be young at heart. Angels???

3DL or 4DL is a choice, which lifestyle do you choose?

Create– *Synonyms*–originate, invent, develop, devise, formulate, make, concoct, contrive, fashion, design, form, mold, erect, construct, bring into being

OR

Create– *Antonyms*–destroy, demolish, annihilate, close, shut down

Scene Twenty-Seven

When to Let Go

Helen's parents have been driving Helen around the countryside in their horse and buggy to confuse her with where she is at. Little does she realize she's just down the path from her home going to the little cottage.

Miss Annie: Does she know where she is?
Kate: No.
Captain Keller: For all she knows, she could be in another town--
Kate: That's her sign for me.
Miss Annie: Yes, I know. In two weeks.
Kate: Miss Annie, I-- please be good to her. These two weeks, try to be very good to her--
Miss Annie: I will. (Helen sobs and fights when she realizes she is with Miss Annie again.) Two weeks. What did I get into now?

In this scene, Mom is learning to let Helen go, even if letting go means being steps away from the main house. Her constant plea, *"Miss Annie, please be good to her."* almost seems as if she's really asking Miss Annie to pity Helen and not to ask or demand too much from her. Any parent would feel concerned about their child, especially a challenged child, as Kate does. Although there comes a time when a parent needs to let go of some of the apron strings and let the child experience their own life's path.

Take a look at the bigger picture of permitting the child to experience what they are here to learn; to be an active participant in their own life lesson. By feeling sorry for a child, by wanting to rescue a child and by feeling generally distressed – these are all reasons to let go rather than pitying the child and their situation; 3DL. The opposite action would be 4DL, honoring the Universe's grand plan. The Universe provides for special opportunities so that we can truly experience life; special opportunities so that we can gain an understanding of the tools our children will need to create the life they are meant for.

———

Possible Miracle Worker Dialog—Context Sensitive

When at a crossroads, realize you can either continue on the current course of events or recognize a time for change is upon you. Kate is hesitant, but Miss Annie is ready for the change. Here are some phrases you can say when you want to assure an individual who may be at a crossroads.

- 'Right now, know that I am doing the right thing.'
- 'You need to trust what I am saying, even though you may not want to hear it.'
- 'Consider what I am telling you.'
- 'Understand, I know what I am doing, and I know what I am saying.'

———

It's a funny thing -- life lessons. Worth repeating…we can make life easy for ourselves or more difficult for ourselves *and* each other. We can value what the Universe is trying to tell us and go with the lesson, or we can fight it. In Helen's case, the Keller family can make her feel justified in her personal plight, and believe there is no hope, or they can encourage her esteem by giving her the self confidence she needs in order to help Helen rise above the challenges. Certainly, esteem and self-confidence are both moral character developments she's dearly going to need for the rest of her life.

Imagine a classroom full of students with at least twenty different personalities. Divinely the Universe has put these students together so they can push each other's Spiritual growth and development buttons. This classroom environment is where they synthesize all their experiences in life so far. Each individual child collects more evidence, struggles through more life lessons and then decides where on the pecking order of life they will hang out. The scale slides from one extreme to the other, from the very popular classmates to the least popular and every personality in between. A parent can't possibly save a child from everyday life unless they plan on sitting in the classroom everyday or worse yet, be employed by the same school so they can all be together. What encouraging words will we use when our child plops into the car complaining about their school day? How will you interact and positively empower the child, build up their self-esteem and self confidence? Or will you simply validate their frustrations and help them to believe that life should be one or more of the following: life is a struggle, life is hard, I hate people, I don't have any friends, I don't like girls, I don't like boys, I don't like authority figures, the teacher is stupid?

Interestingly, when we choose to follow the Universal flow of life, things will fall in line; more successes are naturally and congruently experienced with far less upsets and challenges. Many call this experience synchronicity, the Divine, Divine order, Divine intervention, serendipity, planets that are aligned, karma, or simple coincidence. When we fight the messages, we experience disease, dis-ease – if you will, sadness, depression, confusion, anger, fear, and drama, just to name a few.

What a great tool to use. Simply by observing our children and their struggles gives us the message that we aren't quite lined up with the Universe, and something more needs to be done. What a great opportunity to reconsider life choices and pick another choice. What a great opportunity for us - to see the human drama for what it is - communication. Allowing ourselves to take the time to discern the Divine communication provides for new ideas, new choices, and new options.

Miss Annie has two weeks to make a difference with Helen. Two weeks, how can anyone think they could make a difference, especially with a child as challenged as Helen? Miss Annie is nevertheless determined. I'm sure there were times when she questioned if she was going to be successful or not. Notice her last statement; *"What did I get into now?"* proves some sense of uncertainty. Regardless, Miss Annie trudges on, maybe even a bit naive about the challenges she will encounter. Miss Annie is after all, very young herself, a determined twenty-one year old. Young and dumb - just the ticket necessary to push through the issues!

Remembering back to our school days, the teacher would, yet again, hand out another work sheet on the same math lesson. Then there would be homework to practice more of the same math problems. The math unit seemed to last forever as we diligently work on fine-tuning the lesson. Not an easy task, and certainly not much fun, only to be repeated the next year with a new teacher. Many of the topics and themes in this primer have also been repeated. We need to hear the concept over and over until we truly grasp the information. Much like the math lesson, we forget the majority of what we have learned during the school year, and we just returned from a simple Spring or Summer vacation. So elusive, math escapes us <u>if we don't use it.</u>

The same is true while learning about our life lessons, our Spirit. The Universe is the teacher. She provides us with daily work sheets, although sometimes it feels like moment to moment work sheets. The Universe knows we still haven't perfected the lesson and gives us yet again, another 'work sheet', to practice again, on the same problem. The older we get, the more elusive. The older we become the further away we get from what we knew about our Spiritual self. We've now become a part of the human culture and have lost most memory of our Spiritual self. The 4DL tools we learn will escape us <u>if we don't use them.</u>

When something or some situation is right and in Divine alignment we light up, we celebrate, we walk with a skip, we smile to ourselves, and we experience the 4DL feeling. When something or some situation is not right, recognize this as the result of poor choices and not Divinely-aligned, but ego aligned, we then slump in our chair sulking as we stare off into space, we're sad and depressed. We wonder how life became so difficult. There is no celebration.

Which do you prefer – a celebration or a sulk-fest?

Anna Sweetnam Ph. D.

What a Miracle Worker Would Share

What tools do the Keller family need to work with so they don't fall into the same repetitive pattern when Helen is back in 'two weeks'? How are you proving to be deaf and dumb too? Most often we don't seem to understand the patterns of life we keep falling hostage to. The truth of the matter is we all constantly fall hostage to the familiar patterns of life while overcoming the life lesson. This is the exact reason we are experiencing life -- to work through and overcome life lessons. It is our job, if you will; to fall, to struggle with a life lesson 3DL, and then work toward learning new tools 4DL instead of using the old tools. If we continue using the old tools that don't ever seem to work, why are we then surprised when they in fact don't work, and wonder what the problem could be?

In today's world there are plenty of training sessions, therapy centers and counselors. Go with your gut instinct and research what's available for you and your family; some solutions could be in your very own back yard. The Kellers could have made a huge mistake sending Helen to an institution... what mistakes are you making? Find someone who will teach you how to listen to your Spiritual nudges and lose the ego drama; 3DL. Find a Spiritual Advisor who will help you to master the stages of Transformation in order to grasp and hold on to the 4DL feeling. The following is a list of five stages necessary for true transformation to happen:

Five Stages of Transformation

The first step of Transformation is to **Recognize** the problem. Sometimes it is difficult to see ourselves as we really are. The Universes' constant feedback reveals to us that what we've been doing isn't working, therefore helping us recognize truths. The lesson has not yet been learned. Finally, there comes that time when the mind can no longer fool the heart.

After this initial recognition you are ready for the second step of Transformation, **Ask.** Ask for more information: 'What is really going on?', 'What do I need to do?' Successful clients will actively search for self-help books, talk to a friend, seek out experts and ask how to overcome the stubborn resistance to change. These individuals are ready to take action to prevent dis-ease.

The third step of Transformation is the most difficult. Clients often **Deny** the problem. After all, it's so much easier to deny the validity of the Universe's feedback and resist facing up to anything at odds with the self-image. 'Anything' can also refer to the 'change agent' in the process as well. Clues of this denial tendency include being upset with the change itself, and defending yourself and/or beliefs that don't work. You may consciously want to change but still experience the old way, the 'old pattern'. Blaming the change agent is easier, and more convenient. Unfortunately life then continues to be chaotic. Denial can last two days, two months, two years or a lifetime, but it doesn't have to.

The forth step of Transformation is to **Accept**. Successful clients can accept all changes if they maintain the focus and are determined to tolerate the transitional discomforts while transforming aspects of their own personality and accustomed character traits. Count on losing this focus - it's normal, it's natural. Losing focus means a true healing has not yet been experienced. Embrace losing and reverting to 3DL; this will encourage a 4DL re-focus. The Universe will always throw in a new challenging experience, to test and to determine if you are ready to **Accept** again.

The fifth stage is the actual **Transformation**. At this point, clients understand the 'bigger picture' of life and experience life differently - both consciously and Spiritually. They are fully transformed! From time to time, even transformed clients can derail and fall off the natural path of their life's journey. The difference here is they now realize the need for continued practice as they leave the old patterns behind and process new life experiences on their own. By seeking answers from within, they are accountable and responsible for the life they choose to create - with purpose.

Healing comes in all manner of forms and stages. The real and fully-lasting healing requires time, effort and understanding. This healing allows for shifting paradigms from the old to the new, from 3DL to 4DL. Mostly it's all about reaching in and choosing a different tool in the tool box. The variety of tools to be learned tried and tested are endless. Be determined and open to using the new tool, the new idea. Truthfully a day shouldn't go by without considering what you could learn about yourself. We are all here to recognize, to ask, to push through denial, to accept change and lastly, to transform. Everyday we could ask ourselves 'What is really going on?' The Angels are indeed very proud of you, *"Ahhhh!"*

3DL or 4DL is a choice, which lifestyle do you choose?

Determined– *Synonyms–*decision, determination, resolve, judgment, solution, verdict, conclusion, finding, reasoning, fixing, act of deciding, perseverance, stick-to-it-tiveness, boldness, power

OR

Determined– *Antonyms–*indecision, doubt, instability, hesitancy, hesitation, weakness.

Scene Twenty-Eight

The Original Sin

In this scene Brother Jimmy and Miss Annie have a conversation. Miss Annie labels his attitude of giving up as the original sin.

Brother Jimmy: How will you-- win her hand now, in this place?
Miss Annie: Do I know? I lost my temper, and here we are. I'm counting on her. That little head is dying to know.
Brother Jimmy: Know what?
Miss Annie: Anything. Any and every crumb in God's creation. I'll have to use that appetite too.
Brother Jimmy: Maybe she'll teach you.
Miss Annie: Of course
Brother Jimmy: That she isn't. That there's such a thing as-- dullness of heart, Acceptance. And letting go. Sooner or later we all give up, don't we?
Miss Annie: Maybe you all do. It's my idea of the original sin.
Brother Jimmy: What is?
Miss Annie: Giving up.
Brother Jimmy: You won't open her. Why can't you let her be, have some pity-- on her, for being what she is--
Miss Annie: If I'd ever once thought like that, I'd be dead.
Brother Jimmy: You will be. Why trouble? Or will you teach me?

'Pity', such a strong thread-word throughout The Miracle Worker story and here it reveals itself once again. Doubting Thomas aka Brother Jimmy, visits Miss Annie and Helen at the cottage. Curiously he asks Miss Annie how she will reach Helen now. It seems he's especially curious about why 'this place' would make a difference. If Miss Annie couldn't reach Helen at the house, why would the little cottage work out any better? An interesting question although this is just an example of how we often speak before we've really thought a concept through. We blurt out our doubts and our disbeliefs without consideration of the person we are talking to. It could be that since Jimmy wasn't successful reaching Helen himself, why should Miss Annie be any more successful in 'this place'? The lack of success has propelled the Keller family to have a *'Sooner or later we all give up, don't we?'* attitude.

As an advocate for Helen, this kind of talk doesn't help Miss Annie. Miss Annie has had to listen to all the Kellers and their various give-up attitudes of hopelessness. With all that, Miss Annie has to fully purge the negative energies and beliefs. Miss Annie needs to dismiss the hopelessness and carry on without the influences of those who have apparently given up. *"If I'd ever once thought like that, I'd be dead."* Miss Annie has to focus and rely on her innermost strength, her gut instinct.

What else is left if you give up? Where have you given up? Have you given up on your hopes, dreams, all due to a challenge? Get back up, get back in the game. You have fallen into the easy trappings of everyday human life. These beliefs include: doubt, lack, confusion, disbelief. It's so easy to do, falling back into a hopelessness and despair. Refer back to the Five Transformation Stages (Chapter Twenty-Seven) if you are struggling with discouraged beliefs. Be your own best perfect advocate. It is enough that others might undermine you, do not undermine yourself!

Be aware of the friends or support groups you frequent. Do they lift you up or bring you down? Do they support your beliefs of hope or the doubtful beliefs you continue to hold on to? Do others in the group share their own discouragement thus influencing you in a negative way? Is everyone in the group bonding together with their stories about their dysfunctional wounds? Is there any sense of anyone overcoming the wounds or rather staying stuck in their 'woundology'? Who is holding the group back because they really enjoy staying stuck, enjoy the inappropriate attention, and wish to remain attached to wounds? What about the leader of the group, do they come from a pity platform or do they hold attendees accountable for staying stuck? Even Brother Jimmy suggests: *"Why can't you let her be and have some pity on her for bein' what she is?"* You wouldn't want to find a group of individuals who think like the Keller family. Instead find a new group, find new friends. Find a group where individuals hold themselves accountable and responsible and do the hard, right, thing, the 4DL. However if you don't want to get past being stuck, you will find all sorts of reasons not to find a new group.

Possible Miracle Worker Dialog–Context Sensitive

Miss Annie does a fine job in this scene, of sharing a dialog about standing up to your convictions. We certainly can learn so much from Miss Annie. Take a minute and role-play in your mind with someone who may have a tendency to put you down or to put your good ideas down. What will you say exactly? Keep the dialog fresh in your back pocket. Be prepared to use it or a version similar. The Universe will surely provide an opportunity to try to heal the interaction, again. When something is not healed the Universe will always provide a new opportunity to create a healing. Be aware, connect and see the pattern in order to choose a different response.

Some phrases to keep handy in your back pocket...

- *'That's interesting, do you think so?'* Come from curiosity when you say it.
- *'That's a good idea.'* Use this even if you don't really think so.
- *'Thanks for your advice, I'll think on that.'* Use this even if you don't.
- *'You know, you might be right.'* This doesn't necessarily mean you agree.

You could pick a response that is the opposite of how you would normally respond. You may be a little out of your comfort zone or quite a bit out of your comfort zone. No one likes to be put into a possible conflict situation. Most important of all, do not take the conversation personally.

-*'Tell me more about what you are thinking.'* Helpful individuals may really be sharing their reasons and doubts for why they wouldn't… but somehow you should!

-*'I don't understand, tell me more.'* You may be able to determine genuine concern or personal fears, which has nothing to do with you.

-*'If that was meant to hurt, it worked.'* The word 'you' is not used in the sentence. (If that was meant to hurt YOU did!)

Own and be accountable for what you really want, rephrase, remold, and reframe your thoughts and your words in a way that takes care of you. Consider the result you are looking for and come up with 4DL language to support you. Be your very own best cheerleading self!

What a Miracle Worker Would Share

Miss Annie is trusting that Helen's curiosity about life will prove to make the biggest difference in being able to 'open her up', to 'reach' her. Even little babies reveal their different developmental stages, they too are naturally curious. We are all naturally curious, even if we get lost and fall backwards for a while. 'How far do we fall?' is the question. If one way doesn't work, do we give up or try another way? Miss Annie won't hear of any negative comments, she dismisses Brother Jimmy so he won't influence her any further. Miss Annie closed the doors on Brother Jimmy again, or at least the window shutters!

> *"She learns because she can't help it, just as a bird learns to fly."*
> **Annie Sullivan, The Story of My Life. p267**

Miss Annie understands and trusts that Helen is naturally curious enough about life, just like she was and she continues to be curious about life. She believes Helen is interested in *"Anything. Any and every crumb in God's creation. I've got to use that appetite too."* Miss Annie has to reach that part of Helen's Spirit that yearns to experience life in a healthy 4DL way. The Keller family has virtually given up and don't have any other responses left except to pity Helen. This combination keeps them all firmly entrenched in the 3DL.

Be forewarned about friends and support groups that are only experiencing 3DL. They will drag you down to that level. You may eventually choose not to participate in the group or you may want to find a new group of friends that are encouraging rather than discouraging. Find a support group that advocates and encourages a fourth dimensional lifestyle, 4DL. They won't have to even say the words, 4DL, you will know the difference, and you will feel the differences. As the Five Stages of Transformation share, we all fall back, we lose focus. Is this loss of focus for the group a simple two day loss or a devastating life time loss? Are they meeting their life challenges or are they failing miserably? If you only want validation for your own misery, if you only want your own piece of the pity-party, then this group is for you. If on the other hand, you're ready for the fourth Transformational Stage then you are ready for real change and genuine transformation, so find a new group. This is a choice. *"Ahhhh!"* the Angels love you!

3DL or 4DL is a choice, which lifestyle do you choose?

Advocate— *Synonyms*—recommend, advise, propose, prescribe, champion, urge, promote, plead the cause, argue for, speak out for, stand up for, push for, encourage, endorse, favor, support

OR

Advocate— *Antonyms*—oppose, adversary, combat, attack, assail, opponents, enemy, antagonist, detractor, attacker, accuser

Scene Twenty-Nine

Influenced

In this scene Miss Annie gets quite clever as a means of 'reaching' Helen. Percy is a little boy who stays with Miss Annie and Helen at the cottage. His role is to help Miss Annie if she needs something from the main house.

Miss Annie: *No! No pity, I won't have it. On either of us. (Helen cries out when Miss Annie tries to touch her.) I will touch you! How how? How do I--? Percy! Percy, wake up! Get out of bed and come in here, I need you. Percy? You awake?*

Percy: *No'm*

Miss Annie: *How would you like to play a game with Helen? Touch her hand.*

Percy: *Lemme go! Lemme go-- She tryin' talk. She gonna hit me.*

Miss Annie: *She can talk, if she only knew, I'll show you how. She makes letters. This one is C...C... She's mad at me now though, she won't play. But she knows lots of letters. Here's another, A. C-a-k-e. She spells cake, she gets cake. She doesn't know yet it means this. Isn't that funny she knows how to spell it and doesn't know she knows. Well, if she won't play it with me, I'll play it with you. Would you like to learn one she doesn't know?*

Percy: *No'm.*

Miss Annie: *M-i-l-k. This is M... I... That's an easy one, just the little finger. L is this-- No, why should I talk to you? (Helen becomes curious and moves over to them.) I'm teaching Percy a new word L, K is this-- So you're jealous, are you? All right. Good! So I'm finally back to where I can touch you, hm? Touch and go! No love lost, but here we go. You can go to bed now you've earned your sleep. Thank you. Now all I have to teach you is...one word, Everything.*

"No. No pity. I won't have it. On either of us." This is an incredible insight, so 4DL. Miss Annie won't tolerate pity for Helen nor will she tolerate pity for herself. Pity…it's so easy to fall into. There are so many possibilities and opportunities in life that don't work out. So many upsets and disappointments happen every day. You have them and I have them. Miss Annie won't have them, though. Instead of allowing the current frustrations to spoil Miss Annie's attempts, causing defeat and feelings of despair and depression, Miss Annie instead takes action. How many times have you felt defeated, curling up in a fetal position and feeling depressed, becoming lazy and despondent? Too Many! There you go - doing depression, and all the while looking for someone to show you some sympathy… pity rather, is what we really want. Does anyone notice our 3DL stance? Does anyone care? We want attention, we want someone to notice we are hurt, broken and sad--so 3DL.

How do we get out of this behavior rut? How do we shake off the despair? *Action…* take some action! Do something, anything that might resolve the situation. Having a pity-party for yourself or looking for a pity-party leaves no room for cleverness to discover a good idea or for any idea to reveal itself. *Stop*; take a moment to ask 'What could I do?' Notice and pay attention to the first good idea that comes to mind. Don't dismiss the good idea. Even if it's not something you want to do. It may be something out of your comfort zone, but consider the idea anyway. You may truly <u>need</u> to come out of your comfort zone- to grow, perhaps to grow up?

Here we see a desperate Miss Annie. In the previous scene, Brother Jimmy tried to influence and persuade Miss Annie, and she had to sift through the conversation and hold her course, remaining steady. She just has to stand strong; she has to dig for and listen to her beliefs and to what she remembers from her own experiences having lived and learned them at the Perkins School. After Jimmy announced; *"You won't open her. Why can't you let her be and have some pity on her for bein' what she is?"* Miss Annie becomes a bit desperate and jumps right into action. She wakes Helen up in an attempt to touch her, to reach her. Miss Annie even wakes up Percy to take part in her desperate attempt.

At this point in the story there really isn't anyone who is on her 'side'. There's no one she can look to for support - all great reasons to fall into despair, confusion, depression! Worse yet, Miss Annie has now turned into the family scapegoat. Thank goodness she was able to escape… to the little cottage!

> *"Besides, her past experiences and associations were all against me"*.
> **Annie Sullivan, Story of My Life. P. 256**

Being the family scapegoat is all part of the family pecking order. Miss Annie has not become the reason why Helen is the way she is. It's easier for the family to blame the scapegoat then it is to do the right thing. It's easier to throw Miss Annie 'under the bus' and blame rather than be thrown into this new uncomfortable, unchartered territory and try to survive the changes Miss Annie is introducing. Under these circumstances Miss Annie has no real support system, yet regardless of this Miss Annie has to hang tough - with or without family support. Sometimes, in fact many times, it is best to stand alone and remove the distraction that may make you stray from your good ideas, your course of action. Miss Annie had to take action to prevent the dis-ease. She needed to overcome the overwhelming feeling of being drawn into, literally sucked into, the family pity-party for Helen. In that defining moment, it became time for Miss Annie to take the necessary action as an affirmation and confirmation that Helen could be touched, she could be reached and Miss Annie could indeed make the difference. This difference takes listening, listening to the inner voice guiding you toward the proper action to take. Ask what action needs to be taken in your life. Miss Annie listens earnestly to all that she is, her Spirit, for answers. Listen earnestly to all that you are. You have the answers; dig for them, and you will have them.

Possible Miracle Worker Dialog—Context Sensitive

Sometimes, many times, we may want to have an open dialog with ourselves. We can give ourselves our own pep talk; we could be our own cheerleader, especially when we feel alone, with no one to turn to. What could we say to ourselves? What action steps might we encourage ourselves to take? What strategy could we encourage as if we took a moment to see into the next day or the next week? What would that bit of future look like? What would we want it to look like, and how could we create it? If we think it, we can create it; we just have to take the time to visualize what we ultimately want. Manifest it.

———

Have this type of conversation with yourself; take the time, or like Miss Annie did, journal or write a letter… Even if you don't have the support you need, act as if someone is watching. Someone is truthfully watching, watching from the sidelines, proud of you. Feel that 'someone', feel that energy. Like a secret admirer watching over you, waiting for that precise moment to reach you. Know that this energy is working with you, know that you are supported. Feel the energy of the manifestation and know the Universe is working with you, working behind the scenes aligning with your vision, hopes and aspirations. The good and not so good - it's all aligning.

This is how manifesting works, count on it, expect it. When things don't work out, then realign. Become very clear about your vision of what you want. Remove any confusion, this only confuses the Universe. Remove any doubts; this only creates doubts with the Universe. Remove any clutter, distraction and contrary thoughts that are not in line with your dreams. The Universe will create along with you more and more clutter and distractions in order to move you toward a more fine-tuned version of what you really want. You don't have to experience any doubt, confusion or distractions, just make it perfectly clear to yourself and then watch the Universe support you. It is done! The formula is the same, trust it! It's working now, this very moment…notice what happens tomorrow! The good and not so good-whatever you aligned with, it is done!

Annie wrote wonderful letters to Mrs. Sophia C. Hopkins, the only person to whom Miss Sullivan ever wrote freely. Mrs. Hopkins had been a matron at the Perkins Institution for twenty years. During the time that Miss Sullivan was a pupil at Perkins Mrs. Hopkins was like a mother to her.
The Story of My Life. P, 247.

This activity became for Miss Annie almost like a therapy, writing weekly letters to express the latest events and frustrations to Mrs. Hopkins. Understandably we can validate Miss Annie's frustrations and honor the letters as the chronicled outline of Helen's growth and development.

"Since I wrote you, Helen and I have gone to live all by ourselves in a little garden-house about a quarter of a mile from her home, only a short distance from Ivy Green, the Keller homestead. I very soon made up my mind that I could do nothing with Helen in the midst of her family, who have always allowed her to do exactly as she pleased. She has tyrannized over everybody, her mother, her father, the servants, the little darkies who played with her and nobody had ever seriously disputed her will, except occasionally her brother James, until I came; and like all tyrants she holds tenaciously to her divine right to do as she pleases. If she ever failed to get what she wanted, it was because of her inability to make the vassals of her household understand what it was. Every thwarted desire was the signal for a passionate outburst, and as she grew older and stronger, these tempests became more violent. As I began to teach her, I was beset by many difficulties. She wouldn't yield a point without contesting it to the bitter end. I couldn't coax her or compromise with her. To get her to do the simplest thing, such as combing her hair or washing her hands or buttoning her boots, it was necessary to use force, and of course a distressing scene followed. The family naturally felt inclined to interfere, especially her father, who cannot bear to see her cry. So they were all willing to give in for the sake of peace. Besides, her past experiences and associations were all against me. I saw clearly that it was useless to try to teach her language or anything else until she learned to obey me. I have thought about it a great deal, and the more I think the more certain I am that obedience is the gateway through which knowledge, yes, and love too, enter the mind of the child."

Annie Sullivan, Story of My Life. P. 256

Notice how Miss Annie handles Percy? He says *"No"* to every question Miss Annie asks, he doesn't want to be involved, he doesn't want to help and Miss Annie takes no notice of his responses. Miss Annie is focused; she hangs onto her thread of thought. Here she's trying to get Helen to be comfortable with her touch. She plays Percy against Helen, tries to make her jealous by spending time with Percy. Helen falls for it, another sign that proves Helen connects her dots; even dots about her feelings. She doesn't want to be left out and replaced, Helen wants to be included. Helen may not be able to see or hear, but she does have her other senses.

Particularly important is Miss Annie's following comment: *"Oh, why should I talk to you? I'm teaching a new word to Percy. So you're jealous, are you? All right. Good."* This is a great example of Miss Annie creating invisible check marks in the air. When Miss Annie sees that Helen is jealous, she says *"Good."* Miss Annie understands it is also Helen's anger and frustration that will make Helen take personal action to prevent her own dis-ease. What a great tool anger can be, a great gauge. Anger means we are in the midst of 3DL. Remember, what we really want in life is 4DL feelings. Feelings of joy, love, chills and goose bumps. Anger won't achieve the 4DL goal unless we are ready for change which could be just right around the corner.

Miss Annie is now on her way, discovering Helen's other faculties and senses, all to manipulate as she sees fit in order to 'pop' Helen back into her Spirit. Miss Annie no longer has to deal with the family distractions, now she can focus (listen) and come up with good ideas on how best to reach Helen. Helen's Spirit is constantly crying out and communicating her frustrations. Instead of allowing Helen to respond in the same familiar dramatic way, Miss Annie knows she has to stop Helen in her tracks. She must undo all Helen's beliefs, to make Helen unlearn all that has been learned up to this point that now no longer works. Miss Annie has to make Helen aware that tantrums don't work and that there are other ways and means to communicate. Miss Annie has to help Helen realize and switch to more appropriate ways in order to get her needs met.

"Gradually I got used to the silence and darkness that surrounded me and forgot that it had ever been different, until she came -my teacher- who was to set my Spirit free."
Helen Keller, The Story of My Life. p.5.

What a Miracle Worker Would Share

Miss Annie asks the questions. *"How do I touch you"* Ask for yourself, and if you listen, you will be surprised by the answer that comes to you. You won't hear an answer if you don't ask the question. It can be as easy as asking for a new and different answer or for a good idea to come into your mind. Miss Annie tries a little of this and a little of that, but most importantly she doesn't give up. *"I'm finally back to where I can touch you."* Miss Annie knows she has a long road ahead of her to teach Helen, as she exclaims - *"Everything".*

Use your instincts. Observe the children; what are they trying to say, what are they communicating? The child will tell you if you watch and listen carefully. Think about what it is you expect from the child. Visualize your idea of what a happy, healthy family looks like. Hold that vision in your mind and your heart. Don't lose the 4DL feeling of a beautiful vision of your family. Let this positive energy be felt by others. How could they not feel it with all your attention focused upon it? Manifest it. Miss Annie wasn't always sure which way to handle Helen, but what a positive 'manifester' she became. She held onto the vision of what she expected for Helen. For yourself - be calm, follow your instincts and mostly, hold the energy of the vision you expect as if you were holding the vision in your hand. It's that close, see it in your hand; it's very reachable. Don't let anyone disturb your thoughts. The very act of holding onto this energy of the vision will help your hopes, dreams and aspirations to come true. Reach within, follow your own Spirit, follow and listen to your own gut intuition. Ultimately, trust yourself. The Angels are with you *"Ahhhh!"*

For manifesting purposes, re-read the last paragraph and everywhere you see the word child, put the name of a loved one for whom you hold a certain vision. This can be anyone close to you - a relative, friend or corporate associate; no matter, the information is the same, whether for a little child or adult child.

3DL or 4DL is a choice, which lifestyle do you choose?

Listen– *Synonyms*–attend, hear, make an effort to hear, pay attention, give heed, take notice, note carefully

OR

Listen– *Antonyms*–be deaf to, turn a deaf ear to, ignore, neglect, disregard, take no notice of

Scene Thirty

Championing the Will

In this segment Captain Keller, who holds the most doubts about Miss Annie, takes the time to 'check in' in on the ladies. He doesn't like what he sees.

Captain Keller: On my way to the office, I thought I'd look in on your progress--
Miss Annie: Well, she's tolerating me and I'm tolerating her.
Captain Keller: Where is-- What's wrong?
Miss Annie: Difference of opinion. I think she should dress herself. She thinks she shouldn't.
Captain Keller: Is this her breakfast?
Miss Annie: Yes.
Captain Keller: She wouldn't eat?
Miss Annie: Oh, she'd love to eat it.
Captain Keller: But it's almost ten o'clock. Why haven't you given it to her?
Miss Annie: She understands I will. When she dresses herself. She's thinking it over.
Captain Keller: You intend to starve her into obeying?
Miss Annie: She won't starve, she'll learn. All's fair in love and war, Captain Keller, you never cut supplies?
Captain Keller: This is hardly a war.
Miss Annie: Well, it's not love. A siege is a siege.

Imagine for a moment Captain Keller telling Kate what he just witnessed. I can hear it now, *'Helen is not allowed to eat her breakfast!'* Miss Annie can't catch a break and Helen is not obliged to accommodate... she's not even aware. Miss Annie continues to 'look' bad and incompetent!

Captain Keller can only see the punishment consequence of what Miss Annie is trying to do. *"You intend to starve her into obeyin'?"* I'm sure Captain Keller has used rewards and punishment many times with Helen and I guess it's ok when he uses rewards and punishment, but apparently not for Miss Annie.

Miss Annie has two weeks to coax Helen to tolerate her. If the Captain sees that Miss Annie is holding food back from Helen that certainly doesn't help Miss Annie's situation. Of course, to Miss Annie, she understands the bigger picture of what is going on. She understands her strategy and it's not in the same light as what Dad is looking at. Understandably, it is difficult to separate these two different versions of using food as a punishment strategy. With Dad, you can be sure he would use food as a punishment out of anger and despair. With Miss Annie, food is used as a strategy to win cooperation from Helen. One version is clearly punishment and the other is but a means to an end - an end result that will enable Helen to be raised up from the depths of her darkness.

Reconsider whether or not you want rewards and punishment to be the tools of choice or perhaps let them gently slip down to the bottom of the tool box. Be sure to ask yourself questions about what you think would be the result if you responded this way or that. If I reward, what would be the outcome? Does this improve the relationship or hinder it? What if you use punishment, what message are you trying to get across? Consider using other methods also, like win/win or negotiating. Letting the child have choices is another method. You want to win and so do they, so how will you handle the situation so both of you can win? What suggestions can you draw from each other, what options are available, what choices? Be creative, be playful, and be ingenious while brainstorming together for new ideas.

Remind yourself to be willing to see the bigger picture and remember that the behavior exhibited is a form of communication. When behavior is reasonable, responsible, and age appropriate, the child is communicating to you that all is well in their world. When the behavior is rude, obnoxious, and sneaky without accountability or personal responsibility for what is going on, what are they really trying to say, what is this communication? Don't hold too much stock in the negative behavior. Let the actual negative behavior go for the moment and reach for the important underlying issue.

This will take time, something precious these days, but insist to take the time anyway, and break down the problem. What does the child learn when you take the time to understand and ask questions about what is going on? Jump into their world for a moment, validate their position and be ready to explore options from their perspective in order to resolve the problem. At a later time, when a child is ready to discuss his behavior, remind the child about the particular misbehavior. Discuss other ways of communicating, instead of acting out. Treat them with the respect of a friend who comes to you with a problem over a cup of coffee. Draw out from them some specific solutions; negotiate with them… these are after all, skills they will need to employ in their adult world.

Miss Annie is working with a puzzle in front of her; pieces of the puzzle are literally everywhere. Helen is just about 7 years old and has had ample opportunity to acquire a toolbox full of limited beliefs and limited skills; a bunch of jumbled up puzzle pieces to work with. How do the pieces of the puzzle come together? How can Miss Annie help? What are Miss Annie's strategies and goals? What does a deaf and blind child need? What does any child need? What does an adult/child who acts like a child need? What do any of us need to grow up, what is the goal? What is a parent's goal for their children?

"The greatest problem I shall have to solve is how to discipline and control her without Breaking her spirit. I shall go rather slowly at first and try to win her love. I shall not attempt to conquer her by force alone; but I shall insist on reasonable obedience from the start."
Annie Sullivan, The Story of My Life, p252

—ᴍᴏᴏᴇᴛᴏᴏᴛᴇᴏᴏᴍ—

Possible Miracle Worker Dialog—Context Sensitive

So, in your day to day world, it's time to leave the house to go to the grocery store. You're packing up and making sure you have everything, coupons, money, baby number two... You've already once reminded the three year old to go potty. Now you are ready to leave and you say *'Honey go potty!'* she says, *'I did already!'* You are positive it's not true. Is this an indication of how the morning is going to go - already a power struggle?

4DL response... hand on hip *'No you didn't!'* with a grin on your face.
3DL response... hand on hip *'No you didn't?'* with chagrin on your face.

If you want to witness a big grin appearing on the child's face, matching your grin and even larger as they pass you to get to the bathroom, then I suggest Miracle Worker response 4DL. If you want to witness a pout, indignation and a matching power struggle use the typical 3DL retort! Notice it's all in the hip!!!

—ᴍᴏᴏᴇᴛᴏᴏᴛᴇᴏᴏᴍ—

Miss Annie helps Helen to learn how she can win with her 'teacher'. By relying only on Miss Annie, Helen quickly realizes how she can win as soon as she connects to what Miss Annie is asking of her. Helen can eat her breakfast as soon as she puts on her shoes and socks. For now, using food is the best tool for Miss Annie to use, a tool or 'language' that Helen understands.

"I had made many mistakes, and Miss Sullivan had pointed them out again and again with gentle patience. Finally I noticed a very obvious error in the sequence and for an instant I concentrated my attention on the lesson and tried to think how should I have arranged the beads. Miss Sullivan touched my forehead and spelled with decided emphasis, "Think." In a flash I knew that the word was the name of the process that was going on in my head. This was my first conscious perception of an abstract idea."
Helen Keller, The Story of My Life. P22

For today's Miracle Workers, we want to reach a child through internal motivation and not through external controls, much like the result of reward and punishment. In today's world there is so much emphasis placed upon how many items, toys and things you possess compared to the neighbor. Rewards and punishment feed right into today's beliefs that the winner takes all. Does this attitude really reflect the moral soundness of character we want our children to learn today? Well of course, especially when we want to beat out the neighbors, the Jones. This is apparently so very important to many parents today. We look good on the outside but are actually suffering on the inside. In the 4DL world, we already understand that 'things' don't make us happy. Using reward and punishment and giving 'things' and taking 'things' sets up the child. They begin to learn that 'things', material items, are of great importance in life, they make us happy.

Miss Annie is very limited with her use of manipulative tools to reach Helen, given Helen's handicap. Parents today also use food for reward or punishment as a form of manipulating their children. We can hear rewarding and punishing statements everywhere we go. We could be at the mall, or the beach, and even in church and hear these threats. At home typical threats are: *'Wait 'til your father comes home'* or *'You won't get dessert.'* Or the reward side of *'If you eat all your dinner, you can have dessert.'* Or *'If you pick up your toys, I'll give you two cookies.'*

Miss Annie utilizes food and her intention feels much like a typical threat that parents today would use, but it is quite different. Miss Annie is using the food as if Helen were on the maturity level of a two-years old, waiting for her to get dressed to go to pre-school. For the very first time, Helen is being asked to do everyday tasks that a two-year old would normally do. Parents today unfortunately continue to use food as a manipulation tool whether their child is 3, 4, 5, 9 or 10. It's time for new tools. How will you win your children's cooperation today?

When Helen can truly understand Miss Annie and is operating in an age appropriate manner but still doesn't put on her shoes and socks, then dangling a carrot in front of Helen would have much the same feeling as a parent who continues to abuse the reward and punishment tool. This behavior represents the quick-fix parent style, the same method for any parent who only has a box of band aids in their tool box. This behavior is certainly not the correct or effective solution for parents looking for an end result that reinforces the positive character development of a conscious child.

What a Miracle Worker Would Share

Punishment typically comes from frustration which usually results in yelling and screaming. There is a lot of emotion and anger behind the actual punishment. Taking time to remind the child that rules were either broken or neglected helps to re-establish the limits and boundaries that you as the parent expect. Empathize first, don't immediately use judgment. Try to understand the child's perspective, put your feet in their shoes. What could be some natural consequences for an individual who doesn't follow the rules, who doesn't respect the rules or limits which are designed to ward off and protect from chaos? Not eating breakfast is a good consequence, so is not going outside, until you are dressed.

How does someone with Helen's handicaps ever completely understand why she is left out and why no one in her world seems to understand her circumstances? How does each day come and go and yet she still can't be heard or even validated as an individual with needs? Can anyone really understand her pain and suffering? How does she communicate these needs of being loved, valued, understood, and respected? There are so many questions to consider for someone with Helens handicaps. This is an extremely difficult task even in today's world for today's children who are both seeing and hearing. In today's world, is this difficulty in being heard, of being understood, the beginning point for children who then withdraw and isolate themselves into their own world? Or maybe is this the beginning point for children who constantly act out, begging for inappropriate attention. Where is Mom, where is Dad? Are they together, or are they divorced? Do they have new families, where and how do the children fit in? How do they cope as they hop from one family to the next?

Each family has a unique set of dysfunctional circumstances, and let's just call it what it is, dysfunction. How could it not be dysfunctional, since there are no 'life tools' taught in any school curriculum today? Life tools are just as necessary for learning, and may be even more necessary than today's standard requirements of reading, writing and arithmetic. How many parents take the initiative to search out available resources and consider taking a parenting class? How many parents take a parenting class and risk having family and friends or even the neighbor assume there are problems in their home? Is our own lack of self-esteem or our own pride in the way of a happy healthy productive family? A parent's job is never done. What one thing could you do today to make a difference in your family?

How many adults attend a conflict resolution seminar for surviving office personalities? How many have taken anger management or leadership training as corporate management skills? *Or* who has even taken dog training, an obedience program for the new puppy in the house? Consider the skills learned for a puppy can be equally and incredibly valuable for young children or the adult/child in your life. Imagine!

Now do your part - honor anyone who comes into your life who is willing to share with you the difficult things that need to be shared. Honor this person who is being responsible enough to share with you as your own parents should have. Honor this change agent in your life, let them know you know and understand. Ask for their opinion, their good advice. Open the door to new ideas instead of putting on the brakes. You won't hear the Angels when the brakes are on, they squeal too loud!

3DL or 4DL is a choice, which lifestyle do you choose?

Responsible– *Synonyms*–accountable, liable, answerable, conscientious, reliable, dependable, trustworthy, capable, mature, self-assured, adult, of age

OR

Responsible– *Antonyms*–unaccountable, under no obligation, immature, unreliable, undependable, untrustworthy

Scene Thirty-One

Patience

In this scene Miss Annie has to stand her ground again. No, Mom may not take Helen for a walk!

Miss Annie: *Discipline, discipline, hum. Disinter- disinterested— disjoin—dis--. Disinterested,—disjoin-- Where's discipline? What a dictionary you have to know how to spell it before you can look up how to spell it. Discipl. discipline. dis-cipline!*

Kate: *You're not to overwork your eyes, Miss Annie.*

Miss Annie: *Whatever I spell to Helen, I'd better spell right.*

Kate: *You've taught her so much this week.*

Miss Annie: *Not enough. Obedience is not enough.*
Well, she learned two nouns this morning-- key and water.

Kate: *But-—not--*

Miss Annie: *- No, not that they mean things; it's still a finger game. No meaning. But she will.*

Kate: *Might I-- Might I take her for one walk today?*

Miss Annie: *Shall we play our finger game, Mrs. Keller?*

Kate: *Next week seems so--*

Miss Annie: *Spell it.*

Kate: *So far off.*

Miss Annie: *Spell it! If she ever learns, you'll have a lot to tell each other. Start now.*

Miss Annie knows she's half way there. Helen's parents are ready to accept the merest improvement, expecting nothing more, or maybe because they didn't know Helen's potential. Miss Annie also knows her allotted time is at the halfway point. Miss Annie explains how she knows that Helen is half way there. Knowing that, Miss Annie wants to keep Helen as long as possible. At the same time, Miss Annie has to overcome another sympathetic tug at Helen and not let Kate take Helen for a walk. Should Mom take Helen for a walk, this will no doubt become a distraction and confuse Helen. What would Helen learn if Mom took her for a walk? Miss Annie has come so far with Helen, and there is absolutely no reason to jeopardize the situation now! Unfortunately, there is no training program for Mom - nothing to help her understand how her yearning and need to be with Helen discourages Helen's potential. She is, to put it bluntly, in the way.

Possible Miracle Worker Dialog—Context Sensitive

'When you are involved with and helping a loved one, are you really helping them, or are you helping yourself?' A Miracle will be required to keep this question readily available and easy to reach, at the top of the tool box. Many 'helpers' may not fully understand this key question. What is actually needed here is a shining light to better illuminate your level of comprehension; is the act of helping a loved one really more about whether or not your emotional piggy bank needs filling by being the ever so diligent helper?

The key difference is in the action that took place. The <u>enabling helper</u> positions themselves and gets in the way. Many times they will end up doing what needs to be done, even if the enabled can do it for themselves. The <u>empowered helper </u>encourages, cheers and poses questions along the way. *'How will you handle that? You are clever and I know you will come up with a good idea.'*

Certainly Miss Annie could stand to work with little Helen a bit longer without unnecessary distractions. Mom doesn't empower, encourage or cheer Helen on; Mom just gets in the way.

Notice... this is about Mom's need to be with Helen, this is a 3DL response. Certainly Helen misses her Mom and family. If parents could come from a 4DL understanding even Kate would then allow for Helen to experience this piece of her journey, alone. Mom could sit back and be the observer in Helen's life and cheer from the sidelines. At the very least, send her positive energy, and best wishes and hopes.

For all of us, be patient, remain calm, and stay cool; allow for the learning curve. Maintaining a sense of understanding and calm keeps you from feeling like you are on a life's roller coaster. Exhale, breathe; let life play out. Know the right time when it is important to take the observer's seat and minimize your personal input. Be the student. If there is a need to speak up, you will know—wait for it! Like standing in line patiently waiting your turn, patience means keeping calm and steady. Keep your composure and your reactions to a minimum. Notice, in this state, how life comes to you. Patience…

"…the readiness with which she (Helen) comprehended the great facts of physical life confirmed me in the opinion that as the child has dormant with him, when he comes into the world, all the experiences of the race. These experiences are like photographic negatives, until language develops them and brings out the memory-images."
Annie Sullivan, The Story of My Life, p284.

This fact becomes clear and Miss Annie continues to understand. She seems to summarize on a deeper level the bigger picture of life and the various goings-on of the Keller family. Miss Annie did receive several letters from Kate before she arrived at the Keller home. These first letters from Kate were valuable tools. Miss Annie needed to understand the depth of the job she was about to embark upon. I'm sure she was grateful for any bits of information, any insights into Helen's life from 0 – 7 years old. Any news, any insight prepared Miss Annie for what she was about to experience at her new job.

"Let me sum up a few of the elements that make Helen Keller what she is. In the first place she had nineteen month's experience of sight and sound. This meant some mental development. She had inherited vigor of body and mind. She expressed ideas in signs before she learned language. Mrs. Keller writes me that before her illness Helen made signs for everything and her mother thought this habit the cause of her slowness in learning to speak. After the illness, when they were dependent on signs, Helen's

tendency to gesture developed. How far she could receive communications is hard to determine, but she knew much that was going on around her. She recognized that others used their lips; she 'saw' her father reading a paper and when he laid it down she sat in his chair and held the paper before her face."

Annie Sullivan, The Story of My Life. P341

What a Miracle Worker Would Share

Be as diligent as Miss Annie when it comes to your family, especially your children. Keep your eyes and ears open for new tools that could become more effective than those you are currently using. Don't give up. Watch and observe any third party change agent, be they teachers, a scout leader, friend or family member. Don't fight with your limited experiences and knowledge. It's very possible someone has significantly more answers to your family's problems even though they are not part of the family. What does being a parent really mean? What qualifies you to be the parent expert? What skills or training have you taken upon yourself that would better your family dynamics? Most likely you haven't. The overwhelming feeling of taking on all the family challenges put before you can be almost too much to bear.

Observe any restaurant setting with a handful of Moms, all chatting and enjoying being served rather than serving another meal to their family. Here they are taking a break, relaxing, taking deep breaths with no responsibilities for at least an hour before they are back on parent duty. Listen to their conversations. Eventually the topic turns to the children. The conversation is all over the map. They talk about their frustrations, amazed that the child could have such behaviors. They talk about how they tried this and tried that, they commiserate all on their equally difficult problems; they bond with their stories on how wounded the family is. Like a cat chasing its tail the stories are based on reactive measures, human 3DL strategies. Still, Angels love diligence… *"Ahhh!"*

3DL or 4DL is a choice, which lifestyle do you choose?

Diligence– *Synonyms–*persistence, effort, perseverance, effort, hardworking, earnest, painstaking, careful, thorough, well-intentioned, patient,

OR

Diligence– *Antonyms–*carelessness, laziness, indifferent, erratic

Scene Thirty-Two

Admit it!

Here we see Miss Annie struggling and even doubting her abilities. We all do that, but do we persevere?

Miss Annie: Sewing. Oh, it has a name, and sewing isn't it. E-g-g. Egg. It has a name. The name stands for the thing. Oh, it's so simple, simple as birth. To explain. Helen, Helen, the chick has to come out of its shell sometime. (gasps) You come out too. Thimble. No, not key. Thimble. T-r-e-e. W-a-t...M-i-l...Good girl. D-o-l-l. M-i...) Oh... I feel every day more and more inadequate. My letters must show that I need a teacher as much as Helen. I need help too. Who, who? In all the world there isn't a soul who can tell me how to reach you. How do I reach you?

Miss Annie has removed all the family 'noise' and can concentrate on Helen now, separating herself and staying in the little cottage minimizes the familiar family dysfunction. With the real challenge in front of her, she begins to doubt herself and *"I feel every day more and more inadequate."* Miss Annie admits, *"I need help too."*

"It was no doubt because of this ignorance that I rushed in where more experienced angels fear to tread.
Annie Sullivan, The Story of My Life. P283.

Hindsight! How courageous Miss Annie was! Imagine for even a moment - you have just taken on the challenge of working with a deaf and blind child. Where do you start?

At this point in the Helen Keller story we are moving past the point of handling the distractions caused by the parents. We are moving on from watching Miss Annie fight off the parents and the constant battle of beliefs on how they think Miss Annie should handle Helen. Miss Annie is finally removed from all the 'noise'. There was indeed so much noise Miss Annie had to wade through. Noise that resembles: family doubts, misconceptions, negativity, denial, and especially the family habit of enabling. Miss Annie has escaped everything and anything that was keeping her from reaching Helen with real and honest training and teaching. Finally, Miss Annie can get on with the important issues and concerns of reaching Helen. Finally, Miss Annie can focus without further distractions. No more procrastination; now it's time to roll up the sleeves and get down to the real work. The fun begins!

We've all felt overwhelmed with many of life challenges and not felt quite up to the task in front of us. What are we supposed to do? Do we give up? Yes, much of the time we do give up, many parents give up. Like Miss Annie, what do we do? We carry on, that's what we do. We make mistakes, and we pick ourselves up and try again. We don't give up; we don't give up - ever. These are our children we're talking about. Little human beings who look like us, walk like us and talk like us. Somewhere deep inside of us we truly want the best for our mini me's. Sometimes we just don't know what to do, but this shouldn't be our excuse. If you don't know what to do, go find out! Research, discover, learn to ask questions - lots of questions. Become the expert in the field forced upon you. Truthfully it is our responsibility to instill in our children inner discipline, leading them toward healthy, autonomous productive lives.

Possible Miracle Worker Dialog—Context Sensitive

So there's a challenge - if not dealt with now, when? Deal now or deal later, sooner or later the issue will need to be dealt with. The Kellers understood finally that it was time. If not dealt with, what will the child learn? They'll learn there's nothing wrong with the behavior. It's not often that a parent would have a knock-down, drag-out fight, as Miss Annie had with Helen. When faced with a challenging behavioral situation with your child, simply and firmly ask *'Your behavior tells me this is a bad day. How about we go home, rest up, get a good meal and try another day?'* Be sure to have a consequence of substance so the child will understand the seriousness of the situation. If the child assures you he's OK, then believe it! Chances are the child understands the consequences. They know you are serious, since you have 'followed through' before and will do so again when necessary. You need have no more discussion!

———————

When your children constantly exhibit inappropriate behavior, nothing in your life will work well. Unhealthy families lead to unhealthy parents, unhealthy workplaces, and unhealthy relationships. Everything in your life will become infected. Nothing will go right. Fix right away what is going on in your home; figure out a way to enjoy going home and spending time with your family. Whatever the angst, fix it. Take the appropriate action right away to prevent the dis-ease experienced in your home. Take on the challenge with joy. Learn what you can learn, explore uncharted areas or what would feel uncharted for yourself. Reach past your comfort zone and be excited about learning everything having to do with new behavior tools. Build your self-esteem.

Dare to improve your life, and enjoy the trickledown effect as your children grow. Break the dysfunctional cycle in your family from those same dysfunctions you grew up with. Watch your children be little seed planters influencing their friends and co-workers. Watch your children support each other as larger problems crop up. When your children were young they had small problems. As they grow older your children will experience grown-up concerns and issues. As responsible parents, admit it and take the time necessary to discipline. Start grooming, guiding, redirecting, and actively empower your children with lifelong life skills. The earlier you start the better. Take daily risks exposing your own vulnerabilities, your own lack, and your confusion as a parent - in short, make mistakes. The truth is you are already exposed to others - neighbors, teachers, friends, families already know what kind of character your children exhibit. Everyone knows, but we need an individual like Miss Annie to actually say it!

For Miss Annie, she has to grab from all her past experiences. She can now take the time to think about those resources. In Scene Nineteen we are briefly introduced to Dr. Howe.

Miss Annie: *Oh, there's nothing impaired in that head. It works like a mousetrap.*
Kate: *And... when will she learn?*
Miss Annie: *Maybe after a million words. Perhaps you'd like to read Dr Howe on the question of words.*
Kate: *I should like also to learn those... letters, Miss Annie.*
Miss Annie: *I'll teach them to you tomorrow morning. That makes only half a million each.*

> *"Dr. Howe is the great pioneer on whose work that Miss Sullivan and other teachers of the deaf-blind immediately depend on."*
> **The Story of My Life, p 243.**

> *"The golden words that Dr. Howe uttered and the example that he left passed into her thoughts and heart and helped her on the road to usefulness; and now she stands by his side as his worthy successor in one of the most cherished branches of his work...*
> *Miss Sullivan's talents are of the highest order."*
> **Mr. Anagnos, The Story of My Life, p 248.**

What a Miracle Worker Would Share

It's time to take on parental responsibility, admit it! Don't be ashamed, be a proud parent. None of us have been given a handbook on raising children. There is a lack of social skills training, if any, in schools today. How could you possibly know how to discipline your child in ways that build self-esteem when we, as adults, exhibit minimal self-esteem ourselves? Where do you turn? Where in your community do you look? Just start anywhere - start looking. Reach within; reach down deep to...

> *"Some innate capacity for knowing and doing, which we did not know we possessed until the hour of our great need brought it to light."*
> **The Story of My Life p. 257**

What if we were to admit and confess our failures as a behavior designed to attract more appropriate behavior, even better behavior? Can we take a negative behavior and make a positive affirmation, professing the result we would like to see? How would the Universe accept the energy (((vibration))) of a wildly exciting statement of what is right, or at least almost right, in our world… and act as 'IF'? Notice your own energy (((vibration))) of shaking off and losing the ill feeling of a confession, for a corresponding thrill and chill sensation with the following statement…

Just for today… and maybe for the rest of my life-- I admit it! I admit it!!! I am wildly excited and stoked about the Divine's perfect influence as my life aligns with my true intentions.

Make confessing and admitting easier in life, even when it feels perfectly imperfect. Begin to 'love it that way' and in your own search for perfection, take the next step today - manifest your most cherished desire. You will have to rely and trust your own Spirit for many answers in the most trying moments. This is not much different than relying on your own intuition and gut instinct when you have gone through trying times and resorted to basically 'shooting from the hip' for answers… and this too you survived. Go for it, something must be done. Take action. The child is in pain, the parents are in pain, other children are in pain; don't let this be the ripple effect that will extend out into the world. Do not allow this anger to seep into the world around you just because expectations, standards and inner discipline were not insisted upon. How will the world ultimately measure you and your family; what legacy are you leaving behind? Step up and know the Angels are there to support you. *"Ahhhh!"*

3DL or 4DL is a choice, which lifestyle do you choose?

Admit– *Synonyms–*confess, concede, profess, declare, own up

OR

Admit– *Antonyms–*exclude, keep out, dismiss, reject, deny

Scene Thirty-Three

Half Way is Not an Option

In this scene Captain Keller is pleased enough with Helen's progress, but as expected, Miss Annie is not. It seems that meeting a half way point is not an option for Miss Annie.

Kate: Doesn't she need affection too, Miss Annie?

Miss Annie: She-- never shows me she needs it, she won't have any—caressing or--

Captain Keller: And what would another week accomplish? We are more than satisfied, you taught her things to do, to behave, so manageable, cleaner, more--.

Miss Annie: Cleaner?

Captain Keller: Well. We say cleanliness is next to godliness Miss--

Miss Annie: Cleanliness is next to nothing, she has to learn that everything has its name! Those words can be her eyes, to everything in the world outside her, and inside too, what is she without words?And they're in her fingers now; I need only time to push one of them into her mind! One and everything under the sun will follow. Don't you see what she's learned here is only clearing the way for that? Give me more time alone with--.

Captain Keller: Look. What is she spelling?

Kate: Water?

Captain Keller: Teaching a dog to spell. The dog doesn't know what she means any more than she knows what you mean, Miss Sullivan. I think you ask too much of her, and yourself. God may not have meant Helen to have the... eyes you speak of.

Miss Annie: I mean her to.

Captain Keller: What is it to you?

Miss Annie: Half a week.

Captain Keller: An agreement is an agreement.

195

Miss Annie*: Mrs. Keller?*
Kate*: I want her back.*
Captain Keller*: I'll send Viney over to help you pack.*
Miss Annie*: Not until six o'clock. I have her until six o'clock.*
Captain Keller*: Six o'clock. Come, Katie.*

Notice how Miss Annie is on guard. Helen's parents are throwing out absurd comments to cement their cause. They are desperate to collect evidence about what is wrong or not working out in order to justify why they are right about how Helen will never be reached. Sadly, doing half a job is good enough for the family. Miss Annie hears this absurd logic, the Keller's both resort to more noise and are ready to settle: *"We are more than satisfied."... "You taught her things to do, to behave."... "Cleanliness is next to godliness."... "You ask too much of yourself."... "God may not have meant Helen to have the eyes you speak of."* Miss Annie wants more, even eyes to see - as Miss Annie responds, *"I mean her to."*

Have you settled with your child? Have you become lax with your expectations of the way you would like your children to behave? Have you decided a little slippage here and a little slippage there won't really hurt anything? Ask yourself why you made inappropriate behaviors ok? Why are you allowing and tolerating for slippage? I can promise that you are just at the very start of experiencing the inevitable downward spiral; the operative word here is 'downward'. Is it time to turn the downward 3DL spiral around toward an upward 4DL spiral? There's never a good time to go downward. The Universe manages to contrive all of these challenges as part of the life lessons; you can either deal with the problems as they come up or deal with them later. Somewhere, somehow they will have to be dealt with, maybe eventually by the authorities, if you choose to ignore the messages.

Possible Miracle Worker Dialog—Context Sensitive

Once you realize that enabling and feeding into pity-party frenzies for a loved one never effectively work, then anything else you may do feels like tough love. Take a moment to express your feelings. Start with an apology. *'I made a mistake. The way I showed my love to you wasn't appropriate.'* Then continue, *'Sometimes I feel sorry for you, and when I feel sorry I too do things for you, things you could be doing for yourself. I'm not going to do that for you anymore. I thought I was doing the right thing and now I realize I wasn't. It may seem hard at first and you may feel like I don't care and I don't love you. From now on, you can count on me to encourage and empower you. I will not enable you any longer by doing things that you can do for yourself.'*

What a Miracle Worker Would Share

Rightfully Miss Annie insists upon possessing every last minute of the agreement. Why would Helen's parents take less? It's clear that they can see Helen's improvement. Why would you as a parent expect less? What vision do you have for your family, for your children? Do you even have a vision? What do you see? What do you imagine? Is anyone happy?

Like Goldilocks and the three bears, is your vision of your family a balanced vision? Are your expectations set too high, or maybe your expectations are too hard. What expectations would be just right? What are the hopes, dreams or aspirations for your family? Like a self fulfilling prophecy or like the mirror we explored earlier, what is being reflected back to you? Are you experiencing a healthy vision of the family version you dreamed of, or are you experiencing a disturbing vision that contains little or no thought of what you could envision your family becoming?

Did you give up on your dream? Or maybe you never dreamed. Give yourself permission to dream the most wildly successful thoughts. Be like Pollyanna, think of all those Hollywood versions of dreams, and then create them. Be the director and producer in your family. Be prepared to say "CUT" and change the scene to meet your expectations of the perfect version of life. Decide what you want, decide what you expect. Decide. Then insist on what you want, insist on what you expect... insist!

Every small success builds upon and leads to more successes. Don't give up! Angelllssss! *"Ahhhh!"*

3DL or 4DL is a choice, which lifestyle do you choose?

Insist– *Synonyms*–maintain, state firmly, assert positively, claim, hold, repeat, reiterate, stand one's ground, persist, determined

OR

Insist– *Antonyms*–deny, beg, plead, ask, request

Scene Thirty-Four

One Word

Here we see Miss Annie is desperately trying to break through to Helen. She won't accept less!

Miss Annie: Yes, what is it to me? They're satisfied. Give them back their child and dog, both housebroken, everyone's satisfied. But me, and you. Feel it. Reach, reach. I wanted to teach you-- oh everything the earth is full of, Helen, everything on it that's ours for a wink and it's gone, and what we are on it, the-- light we bring to it and leave behind in—words /why, you can see five thousand back in the light of words, everything we feel, think, know, and share in words so not a soul is in darkness, or done with, even in the grave. And I know, I know, one word and I can-- put the world in your hand-- and whatever it is to me, I won't take less! How…How do I tell you that this-- means a word, and the word means this thing, wool? Or this-- S-t-o-o-l means this thing, stool?-. Dress. F-a-c-e. Face. (clock striking) M-o-t-h-e-r. Mother.
Kate: Let her come!

Miss Annie has a few precious hours to work with Helen. She is so close to opening up Helen's world. Miss Annie knows about *"words as light"*, AND *"Everything we feel, think, know and share in words so not a soul in darkness…"* What does Helen see through her eyes? Of course, Helen's world is dark.

"Dear child, her restless spirit gropes in the dark. Her untaught, unsatisfied hands destroy whatever they touch because they do not know what else to do with things."
Annie Sullivan, The Story of My Life, p252

Miss Annie knows beyond a shadow of a doubt there's not a soul left in darkness - if they have words. Precious time is slipping away. Miss Annie achieved so much in the two weeks she had with Helen and now it's slipping away like water in the palm of your hand. How can Miss Annie squeeze the most out of the remaining moments she has left with Helen? If Miss Annie is forced to stop now, will Helen ever learn to live independently, autonomously?

What dedication and sheer determination Miss Annie demonstrates. *"And whatever it is to me, I won't take less... How... How do I tell you that?"* Even Miss Annie isn't sure why she's so determined, but she is. Miss Annie knows if she could get Helen to understand even just one word. *"But I know. I know one word and I can put the world in your hand."*

It's almost as if Miss Annie has a vision of Helen walking around using her signs, the hand alphabet, enjoying dinner conversations with her family. Miss Annie could see and hold the vision in her mind's eye. We could give Miss Annie at least the credit for not giving up. What an incredible amount of determination and an equal amount of patience. What gives an individual that inner strength, the fortitude to continue on without wavering? Is it the vision you hold in your mind of what could be? Is this the same as manifesting? Is it this vision, dream or goal that you have guiding you to reach for all of your energy and stamina in order to see the dream come true? Does this amount of determination give you that giddy 4DL feeling? Yes! - this is exactly what it takes; creating a dream, and then visualizing and holding the delightful dream in your mind's eye and doing absolutely everything you can to see the dream come to fruition.

Look at the amount of opposition Miss Annie had to deal with from Helen's family, and she still trudged through and accomplished one goal at a time. What ideas, dreams and visions do you hold for your family? Have you ever considered what success would mean for your family? Could it then hold true, this idea of a vision coming to fruition just as you saw it might perhaps even be better than you envisioned? Your manifestation 'took hold' if you will.

—◦◦◦◦◦◦—
Possible Miracle Worker Dialog- Context Sensitive

How sad to think there are answers, several easier answers to our challenges if we only knew the difference between reaching a child on a 3DL human reactive level as compared to a 4DL Spiritual, intuitive level which reaches the child internally. There are simple explanations for the difference in parenting styles. For example, instead of telling a child what to do and when to do it, why they should and where they should do it, make the effort to flip this 3DL response to a 4DL response and diligently draw out from the child's Spirit pointed questions about when, where, who and how about a given situation. Use these start up questions or statements to learn more about how they see the situation. Remember to come from curiosity…

- 'How does that work?'
- 'Explain to me when…
- 'Share with me who will be there?'
- 'Tell me more, I don't understand.'
- 'How will you manage…?'

From this point, then negotiate what works for you and what doesn't work for you. Shoot for the win/win. Like you, they want to win too. Find some mutual ground to meet on. Allow for brainstorming, good ideas or other possible options. Be diligent, be curious. You will know the right questions to ask when you are clear about the direction you want to go. Be amazed about what wonderful ideas can be conceived when you work and play with new options together. Remember - it doesn't always have to be <u>your</u> way!
—◦◦◦◦◦◦—

What about the opposite effect? What if you can't seem to conceive of the vision or an inkling of an idea of what a successful family would possibly look like? Maybe you've never thought about it. Does that mean you would manifest more chaos and confusion in the family? Your days would be full of seemingly random-type situations that just happen to come your way. The good and the not so good, anything could happen, anything is possible, but definitely not directed toward any given hopes, dreams or aspirations. Life would just happen automatically, and that would be your reality, with no expectations attached. How successful would Miss Annie have been if she lived like that- like Brother Jimmy suggested? *"You won't open her. Why can't you let her be and have some pity on her for bein' what she is?"*

Before Miss Annie arrived we saw the results of Helen's behavior when there wasn't an adult holding a vision of Helen's <u>expected</u> behavior. There was only chaos, and quite a lot of it.

"One thing that impressed everybody is Helen's tireless activity. She is never still a moment. She is here, there, and everywhere. Her hands are in everything; but nothing holds her attention for long".
Annie Sullivan, The Story of My Live, P 252.

What a Miracle Worker Would Share

Take a moment to visualize setting up an altar in a special area in your home, preferably by a window. Maybe there is a small table you can put a scarf, a cloth, or altar cloth. Make the space special, a little retreat, a place you can go to contemplate. Look around for some candles and maybe you have some incense in the house. Place your favorite things there, something that inspires you. Favorite quotes, books you cherish, a family photo with delicious memories. Through the years maybe you collected things, a feather, a shell or a lucky penny... See your new altar with a comfy chair placed by a window, a place where you can relax and enjoy some soft music. Now that you have visualized this special place you can create it. With intention, a family altar can certainly alter your family.

Make a point each morning to take some time to sit at your altar. Enjoy looking out the window sipping on a fresh brewed cup of coffee or steep a flavored herbal tea, something warm and comforting. Notice what you see out the window... let the movement of the blowing leaves and tree branches rock you into a calm relaxed state and just allow yourself to dream.

Dream, dream of the perfect family you want. What would you like for your children? Let's come up with some words and narrow down what one specific word can represent how best to make the family different.

Healthy, autonomous, independent, successful are some good examples that come to mind.

If we truly want our children to become independent and autonomous, then we must teach them that they only need to look to themselves for approval. They don't need to look outside of themselves to you, a teacher or a significant other. They must trust and rely on their own instincts. If they do not, then they are experiencing the antonym for autonomy, which is – dependence. Is that within your vision of what you would like for your children? It would be very much the same as if you were dependent on your children in order to fill your own emotional piggy bank… Hmmm, darn that mirror! Another choice… Synonym or antonym - 4DL synonym or 3DL antonym?

3DL or 4DL is a choice, which lifestyle do you choose?

Autonomy– *Synonyms–*for autonomy is: independence, freedom, liberty, self-determination, self-government, self-rule, sovereignty

OR

Autonomy– *Antonyms–*dependence

Scene Thirty-Five

An Alliance

Miss Annie receives her first paycheck from Captain Keller, and he is impressed. Miss Annie is not, and shares her concerns with the Captain.

Miss Annie: (knocking) Come in.
Captain Keller: Miss Annie, your first month's salary. With many more to come, I trust. It doesn't pay our debt for what you've done.
Miss Annie: I taught her one thing, No. Don't do this, don't do that--
Captain Keller: It's more than all of us could, in all the years we...
Miss Annie: I wanted to teach her what language is. I know without it to do nothing but obey is-- no gift, obedience without understanding is a blindness too. Is that all I've wished on her? No, no. Maybe. I don't know what else to do. Keep doing what I've done and have-- faith that inside she's-- That inside is waiting, like water underground. You can help, Captain Keller.
Captain Keller: How?
Miss Annie: The world is not an easy place for anyone, I don't want her just to obey but to let her have her way in everything is a lie, to her, I can't-- And I don't even love her, she's not my child! Well. You've got to stand between that lie and her.
Captain Keller: Agreed. Won't you come now, to supper?
Miss Annie: Yes. I used to wonder how I could earn a living.
Captain Keller: Oh, you do.
Miss Annie: I really do. Now the question is can I survive it!

Helen and Miss Annie leave the cottage much sooner than Miss Annie would have liked. Everyone is back home in the old environment. What could that mean exactly? Back home, old environment - same people, same responses, with the same old results? Captain Keller is too quick to respond, *"Agreed. Won't you come now to supper?"* What is the Captain acknowledging exactly? Is he too quick to agree because his tummy is rumbling and he's hungry, dinner is ready! Does Captain Keller really have even the vaguest idea of what Miss Annie is talking about when she's trying to create this alliance, his needed support in making sure Helen doesn't regress? Probably not. Where is the necessary training available for the parents in order to tag team with Miss Annie? What new and different tools will they use, or even be capable of using, when Helen comes home?

If they use the same old responses, you can bet the family will continue to get the same old results from Helen. Sure enough, at the first family get-together Helen acts out and tests what she can get away with. *"To let her have her way in everything is a lie."*

March 28, 1887: *"Helen and I came home yesterday. I am sorry they wouldn't let us stay another week; but I think I have made the most of the opportunities that were mine the past two weeks."*
The Story of My Life. p 261

March 28, 1887: *"Of course, it is hard for them. I realize that it hurts to see their afflicted child punished and made to do things against her will. Only a few hours after my talk with Captain and Mrs. Keller (and they agreed to everything), Helen took a notion that she wouldn't use her napkin at the table. I think she wanted to see what would happen. I attempted several times to put the napkin round her neck; but each time she tore it off and threw it on the floor and finally began to kick the table. I took her plate away and started to take her out the room. Her father objected and said that no child of his should be deprived of his food on any account.*
The Story of My Life. P.262

There is always an opportunity for you to respond with the old world view, with ego and doubt or the new view that you've just learned using a sense of strong conviction, beliefs and esteem, 4DL. Observe for yourself this Universal Law playing a role in your daily life. Here's an example; Let's say you found a Spiritual Center in your neighborhood that offers Spiritual growth and development headed by a Metaphysician whom you heard was very knowledgeable. A little nervous and unsure what a session with a Doctor of Metaphysics would look like or feel like, you muster up the courage and decide to schedule a session anyway. You've experienced some recent life challenges and it sure would be nice if you could get some of your questions answered about what the heck is going on. Why certain things happen the way they happen, spinning out of control, complete with the feelings of being let down and discouraged, maybe even a little depressed. Surely there is someone who could shed some light about life disappointments.

Possible Miracle Worker Dialog—Context Sensitive

This is an example of a session with a Metaphysician. A client shares her experience: 'Wow, was that an understatement. I was virtually blinded by the light that was shed. Amazing beliefs and viewpoints I had never considered before. My BS or belief system as the good Doctor explained was completely flipped, over and over. I had to pick up my jaw from the floor several times. I kept hearing myself saying 'OH?!' the entire time' (OH?! –is a sure sign of the shift from one belief to another. Remember as you begin to grasp new ideas there is usually that question mark which represents the confusion of the shift, followed with an immediate exclamation of 'I get it!' Almost as if to say; 'I never thought of that before.')

After a few pointed questions, the Doctor gave me virtually an hour of revealing tools for my tool box. She said I already had the tools; everyone already has the tools necessary for a productive and successful life. Many of these tools are just at the bottom of the tool box rusty and dusty from lack of use. These unused tools confuse us, we aren't very sure how to use or handle them, and they throw us out of our comfort zone. No one can force us to use them, but we might as well consider the idea of selecting a different type of tool for the 'project'. The good news is we don't have to run to Home Depot to get it!

I must say, there were a few 'heads up' comments made by the good Doctor just as we were beginning the session.

- I was told it was up to me and only me to make the necessary changes in my life… *if* I wanted to!
- I was told about the BS shifts from 3DL to 4DL, which was repeatedly pointed out throughout the session.
- I was also warned about the Divinely Orchestrated 'wrench/ opportunities' that would show up immediately, sometime during my day, or during my week, called The Law of Opportunity.
- She told me to take the best and leave the rest.
- She also displayed three hard stock pieces of paper, each with a light bulb drawn on them. The first had a 25watt bulb on it, and the second contained a 50watt bulb, followed by a 100watt bulb on the last paper. She asked me what level of light I would like her to shed upon the topic. She said she wouldn't share the information if she felt it was a 100watt concept, until she got my permission first.

She was true to her word.

Much of the conversation was spun around the issue of abandonment, a concept difficult for me to consider, since my parents are still married, and I was the baby of the family. That just didn't seem to compute, so I thought I would leave that one. So I guess this wasn't a great start. I was fighting the information presented, since I didn't feel there would be much need for change in this area, and yes, it was definitely a 100watt piece. The Metaphysician could feel my hesitation, confusion and doubts which brought out my 3DL. I seriously doubted the 'wrench/ opportunity' around the issue of abandonment since I really felt I didn't have any abandonment issues. Interesting to a point, but not a great session, I was still feeling a little depressed and I was told to process the topics that were touched on.

Well, let me tell you what happened! The following Monday, I went to work trying to let go. I tried to relax a little more as was suggested in my session. That sent me into a tail spin. Can you say 'abandoned'? Thinking and processing my years of growing up… I finally acknowledged I was in fact abandoned. Not in the traditional sense since my parents were still together; this was in the non-traditional sense, once I actually sat still long enough to ponder. In the process of pondering I gave myself my own 100watt light bulb. Since I was the youngest of four siblings, I always had a great deal of attention. Like a new little kitten, I was constantly pawed at, dressed up, picked up, twirled, and played with. As I acknowledged to the good Doctor on my second session (You bet I called for a second session – I was just discovering about the Universe's Laws and I needed a better grasp! I was learning about ME!). Eventually of course, to continue the metaphor, I grew into a full grown cat. I wasn't as fun to play with and even worse my older siblings had their own grownup lives to lead. They went to high school, they had part time jobs, they had boyfriends and girlfriends and other friends, and they drove a car like adults. They left for football games; they left for Homecoming and Prom… Me??? - I stayed home! Left behind - again!

You can only imagine what I learned during my second session. You bet I scheduled another appointment, I was learning all about ME! I was discovering and having an intimate relationship with ME, someone I didn't really know! Like a mirror… I abandon myself - *ewww*, that 100watt bulb stung a bit. The good news is I now have the tools needed to create my life anyway I want, and I discovered 4DL is a much easier way to live! Spending time with a Spiritual Advisor was the best thing I have ever done for myself. Developing an intimate relationship with me, myself and I was the best gift I could ever give - myself. Life is not as complicated as I had been making it. In fact it's very easy, easier once I understood and grasped the bigger picture. Now I just need to learn to continue to hold on to it, like a hand full of water!!!"

The Angels love all of us consciously connected learners, *"Ahhhh!"*

What a Miracle Worker Would Share

What an amazing Universe we live in. Everything moves. The earth moves, the sun moves, and the moon moves. Wind moves the trees and bushes. Hurricanes and tornadoes move. We move, we drive, we fly and we breathe. Everything is moving; everything is energy in motion.

Talk to a scientist and they will tell you your coffee table is energy and it moves too.

In earlier scenes of <u>The Miracle Worker's Primer</u>, there was talk about the symbol of a mirror and how it reflects back to us our thoughts and beliefs. This is more than just more energy, this is a Universal Law. There is another form of energy to contemplate, another Universal Law, the Law of Opportunity. This Law is about how the Universe constantly tosses in a 'wrench', for your growth and development. Amazingly, from a personal perspective when there is a conscious connection, a shift in perspective, a change in beliefs, it's as if the Universe says *'Oh, no you don't. I'll show you.'* Whatever the shift is about, you can bet the Universe will toss in a wrench - or as Miracle Workers like to say, an <u>opportunity</u>. This opportunity is centered upon sending you into a situation in order to force you back into your old beliefs and perspectives. A test, a challenge if you will that says *'Let's test them out to see if they really got it.'* The goal for you? <u>Persevere</u>...Angels *"Ahhhh!"*

3DL or 4DL is a choice, which lifestyle do you choose?

Acknowledge– *Synonyms*–recognize, accept, admit, own, own up to, confess, allow, grant, concede, concur, yield, assent.

OR

Acknowledge– *Antonyms*–disclaim, repudiate, reject, renounce, contradict, deny, disavow, ignore, disregard, disdain, slight

Scene Thirty-Six

Breaking Old Habits

Helen is home and instantly reverts back to old behaviors. This is a critical point for the entire Keller family. Miss Annie recognizes she cannot accept or tolerate any behavior that gives Helen the message that it's OK and there is nothing wrong, even if it is as mundane as napkin etiquette at the dinner table!

Kate: *Miss Annie, it's a very special day.*
Miss Annie: *It will be, when I give in to that.*
Kate: *Please. I've hardly welcomed her home.*
Miss Annie: *Captain Keller.*
Captain Keller: *Oh. Katie, we-- had a little talk. Miss Annie feels if we indulge Helen in these—*
Aunt Ev: *It's only a napkin. It's not as if it were breakable!*
Miss Annie: *And everything she's learned is? Mrs. Keller, I don't think we should—play tug-of-war for her, either give her to me or you keep her from kicking.*
Kate: *What do you wish to do?*
Miss Annie: *Let me take her from the table.*
Aunt Ev: *Oh, let her stay, my goodness, she's only a child; she doesn't have to wear a napkin if she doesn't want to her first evening--*
Miss Annie: *And ask outsiders not to interfere.*
Aunt Ev: *Out- Outsider, I'm the child's aunt!*
Kate: *Will once hurt so much, Miss Annie? I've --made all of Helen's favorite foods, tonight.*
Captain Keller: *It's her homecoming party, Miss Annie.*

Helen reverts back to her old habits. Here goes Miss Annie once again, fighting for Helen. They have come so far and at the very first

210

opportunity, Helen tests the entire family at the dinner table. How cute, the Law of Opportunity, and we're talking about a napkin again. This is very similar to the tale's original breakfast scene. It's as if Helen, who even in her deafness and blindness, understands that the napkin is the perfect button to push!

Mom has made all of Helen's favorite foods. *"It's her homecoming party, Miss Annie."* This is just more noise from the parents that will ultimately serve to hold Helen back. A frustrated Miss Annie stands strong with her standards, insisting that she needs to take Helen away from the dinner table. Miss Annie needs to stand strong and firm. At the same time, Helen needs to know Miss Annie won't let her get away with even an inch of poor behavior. There can be no slippage from the new standards of living just learned in the little cottage. They have come too far to allow for a regression. Notice the words from the prior paragraph: *'fighting for'* Helen, and not *'fighting with'* Helen.

Miss Annie always has Helen's best interests at heart. Miss Annie has certain expectations for Helen and more importantly, Miss Annie knows Helen can do it. Although changing to new behaviors, more appropriate behaviors for children can appear to happen in a relatively short amount of time. None of these better behaviors will 'stick' unless the parents act consistently from day to day to keep unwanted behavior from returning. Quick fixes, denying and avoiding are the old 3DL methods,

"And I don't intend that the lesson she has learned at the cost of so much pain and trouble shall be unlearned. I shall stand between her and the over-indulgence of her parents. I have told Captain and Mrs. Keller that they must not interfere with me in any way. I have done my best to make them see the terrible injustice to Helen of allowing her to have her way in everything, and I have pointed out that the processes of teaching the child that everything cannot be as he wills it, are apt to be painful both to him and to his teacher. They have promised to let me have a free hand and help me as much as possible. The improvement they cannot help seeing in their child has given them more confidence in me."
Annie Sullivan, The Story of My Life, p.262

When we 'fall back', recognize that this is all part of the earlier addictions and definitely not a result of transformation. Falling back doesn't mean you are in the clear from old habits or addictions. Much more effort in the form of education, growth and development is needed. Shifting your BS is not complete-- yet. For drug addicts and alcoholics you hear the term-- they *'fell off the wagon.'* This is nevertheless the perfect time to regroup, to pick yourself up, try again. Recognize the falling back into 3DL thinking and doing. Is this the standard you want for yourself? Initially you may feel the comfort and ease of falling back upon familiar patterns, to a way of life you're most comfortable with. The push toward a fourth dimensional lifestyle, 4DL, might initially appear more challenging - after all this is uncharted territory for you. What will you do? Do the easier choice, or pick the better choice?

Possible Miracle Worker Dialog—Context Sensitive

Are you unsure when certain behaviors are crossing the line and reverting back to old habits? Ask yourself this simple little phrase –*'Appropriate or Inappropriate?'* Ask the family member who has decided to slip into a wayward phase of living – *'Appropriate or Inappropriate?'* Repeat this simple little phrase especially if there is 'noise', hesitation or confusion. Repeating a theme, thought or sentence can be a very effective tool to stay on topic. The answer to this question will guide you toward recognizing the next step that needs to be taken, most likely immediately.

What Transformational Stage is the Keller family experiencing at this point in the story? The fourth stage - the stage that encourages you to *Accept*.

The fourth step is to <u>*Accept*</u>. Clients can accept all types of changes if they maintain their focus and be determined to tolerate the transitional discomforts, while allowing for the transforming aspects of their own personality and character traits. Count on losing this focus somewhere along the way. Losing focus simply means a true healing has not been fully experienced, yet. Embrace the act of losing focus, this will prod and encourage you to focus. The Universe will always throw in a new challenging experience, to test and wonder if you are ready to fully *Accept* now.

Clearly, true transformation is not here for the Keller family yet. But as miracles would have it, the Miracle Worker is close by!

What a Miracle Worker Would Share

Don't we just love Divine interventions! Divinely orchestrated, here we are once again, at the dining table, with the entire family and everyone is failing miserably with the changes they wish to see. The family's wrench/opportunity is right in front of them. They have come so far and at the very first opportunity Helen tests the entire family by making the napkin the issue. As mentioned before, The Law of Opportunity is right there with them, at the dinner table. How cunning Helen is to make a stand by using the napkin. There are no co-incidences.

How about those interventions? Must we wait for the Divine or can we, should we, set up one of our own? Personal interventions are the ultimate gesture of love, caring and resourcefulness. Let's take an example of something we have all experienced, an outing to the park. The last visit to the park didn't go so well. There was crying, mood swings, and an overall crankiness from the children. Makes you wonder why you bother, why make the effort - after all parks are fun! There is a general hesitation to want to go again. So instead - set the stage, set up the intervention. Let the children know it's a park day. Making a genuine attempt, be prepared to leave the park at a moment's notice when the behaviors acted out become intolerable and begin to head home. You may still be in the car heading to the park when the behaviors go awry, turn around. You may have unpacked at the park, pack back up.

This is more of a test for you. Calling it, determining what is acceptable behavior and what is not acceptable. When the children realize what's going on and complain and whine let them know. Share with them… *'I noticed today wasn't a good park day, maybe another day.'* As with any intervention, with the personal admittance of poor behavior the children may beg and promise to behave. Let them know… *'That would be great, next time.'* All the while you are obviously headed home.

What a wonderful example, something that can easily be adapted to whatever is going on in your home or situation. Now let's take one more step... Ask the children, on another day, if they would like to go to the park. Now is the perfect opportunity/challenge, to remind them and ask them what behavior is expected. Follow this conversation up with *'...and what are the consequences if there is acting out???'* *'We go home!'* they cry resoundingly.

Looks like passing grades for everyone, lesson learned. When and if the children decide to 'test' on the next opportunity, how easy for you to calmly, purposefully turn around and go home. Without a word.

What other tools do parents need to work on so they don't fall back into the same pattern, the fourth stage of transformation? How are you proving to be deaf and dumb? Are you tired, at your wits end? Do you know something needs to change? In today's world there are plenty of life skills trainings available for you to research. Go with your gut instinct, research what's available; some program could be in your very own back yard. The Kellers could have made a very big mistake sending Helen to an institution... what mistakes are you making. Doing nothing is a mistake, especially if you <u>always</u> do nothing. There are no more excuses; there are just too many resources available for you. Start today. Your personal success and your families success depends on it. Know you are not alone, Angels--*"Ahhhh!"*

3DL or 4DL is a choice, which lifestyle do you choose?

Standard– *Synonyms*–requirement, specification, guideline, principle, prototype, measure, yardstick

OR

Standard– *Antonyms*–abnormal, different irregular, unusual,

Scene Thirty-Seven

Constantly - A Test

Still at the dinner table, Miss Annie argues with the entire Keller family for Helen's sake.

Miss Annie: She's testing you. —You realize?
Brother Jimmy: She's testing you.
Captain Keller: Jimmy, be quiet. Now she's home, naturally she...
Miss Annie: And wants to see what'll happen. At your hands. I said it was my main worry.
Captain Keller: But she's not kicking now--
Miss Annie: And not learning not to. Mrs. Keller, she'll live up to just what you demand of her and no more.
Brother Jimmy: She's testing you.
Captain Keller: Jimmy.
Brother Jimmy: I have an opinion, I think I should--
Captain Keller: No one's interested in hearing your opinion.
Miss Annie: I'm interested; of course she's testing me. Let me keep her to what she's learned and she'll go on learning from me. Take her out of my hands and it all comes apart. (Miss Annie sits again) Be bountiful. It's at her expense. Please pass me more of-- her favorite foods.
Kate: Take her, Miss Annie.
Miss Annie: Thank you.
Captain Keller: I'm afraid you're the difficulty, Miss Annie. Now I'll keep her to what she's learned, you're quite right, but I don't see that we need send her from the table. After all, she's the guest of honor. Bring her plate back.
Miss Annie: If she were a seeing child, none of you would tolerate one--
Captain Keller: Well she's not; I think some compromise is called for. Bring her plate, please! Occasionally another hand can smooth things out. There. Now, shall we start all over?

This is the moment to gain ground with Helen - or virtually lose everything the Keller family has worked so hard for, especially Miss Annie and Helen. To allow Helen to think that she could eke by even an inch, some level of inappropriate behavior, would be taking steps backwards. You may have noticed even your own children will look over their shoulder to see if you are watching them as they perform an unacceptable behavior. You may have noticed even in your place of employment individuals looking over their shoulder to see if they are being watched. Maybe you look over your shoulder. This is not a sign of a balanced individual, secure within themselves. If you are looking over your shoulder, you're looking to see if anyone else is looking at what could be appropriate, but most likely inappropriate behavior.

Miss Annie tried to explain her biggest fear, Helen's regression back to old habits. *"She'll live up to what you demand and no more"*. We all live according to what is demanded of us and no more, especially when we are young and have everything provided for us. There is no level of expectation; there is no learning curve for taking care of ourselves; how to take out the garbage, sweep the floor or how to prepare a meal. We have been robbed of the simplest of tasks, and most likely rob our children as well. We rob them of their creative talent, their cleverness and the ability to connect the dots between the heart and mind - their Spirit.

How can any of us ever begin to know what we really want when someone else is always around to rescue and fix whatever our needs are? How could we ever possibly dream about the future especially when we are told what to do, when to do it and why! There is no need to think, do, dream, create; we are deaf and dumb.

Possible Miracle Worker Dialog—Context Sensitive

Someone we know who is near and dear to our heart is in the process of giving up. They may be giving up trying to tie their shoe, even when they successfully tied it yesterday. They may give up trying to get out the door with everything they need for the day. They may give up trying to pursue a dream they have sought for all their life. Someone around you is giving up! Validate… *'That looks difficult, if you need help let me know!'* and be sure to walk away. Leave the loved one with the problem, don't worry that they may cry, yell or even swear, keep walking. When they know they won't be rescued they will eventually accomplish the task without thinking that a loud enough tantrum will get you to do what they should be doing for themselves anyway. Free yourself up, free them up and leave the issue with the one who needs to be responsible for it. 'You're clever; I know you can figure it out'. For some you may have to be as bold as *'Do it anyway!'*

———————————

Miss Annie's hands are tied; she can't fight the entire family. Captain Keller just accused Miss Annie. *"I'm afraid you're the difficulty, Miss Annie."* You can just imagine the wind being sucked out of Miss Annie! She gave it every effort, many tries, but sometimes it's important to stand back and let the Universe play its hand. This is definitely a tool in the toolbox. Watch and observe. For many, we always watch and observe to a fault. Find the balance, find the threshold of when to push and when to watch, especially if you know you've done everything you could. Know that the grand Universe's plan is working behind the scenes, supporting the life lesson. Listen to your Spirit to take an action or observe an action. Just be sure that when you listened, it was really your heartfelt Spirit, and not that ego thing.

"Knowledge is power." Rather, knowledge is happiness, because to have knowledge- broad, deep knowledge- is to know true ends from false and lofty things from low. To know thoughts and deeds that have marked man's progress is to feel the great heart-throbs of humanity through the centuries; and if one does not feel in these pulsations a heavenward striving, one must be deaf to the harmonies of life."
Helen Keller. The Story of My Life. p82

What a Miracle Worker Would Share

Find the balance. Your job is to participate and help out as much as you can, support the Universe and like a mirror, the Universe will support you. Notice a heavy sigh when you let go, this is referred to as a recognition reflex, revealing ultimate frustrations. Reflexes can also indicate ultimate success. Witness other recognition reflexes from sighs to foot twitches or small leg kicks - the same kind of kick you make when your Physician taps your knee for a reflex check. As if your body is muscle testing itself, looking for a reflex.

Watch for a body twitch that indicates you are uncomfortable about what is going on; something is off balance. This may be one of those times when you shouldn't help out or intervene. Your mind tries to fool your heart but your body says otherwise. Like body language, listen, watch and feel what your body is trying to tell you. This could be your signal, a sign to sit back a bit, watch and observe the Universe in action.

Be ready, the Universe is setting up for the next opportunity/challenge. You can never make the horse drink the water. Miss Annie couldn't get the Keller family to 'get' it. What to do? Allow the Universe to step in, allow for the conflict, confusion and chaos. Let the next step happen; trust the next step, trust you will know what to do when the time presents itself. Know when to go to the well! Now you're getting it, Angels--*"Ahhhh!"*

3DL or 4DL is a choice, which lifestyle do you choose?

Balance– *Synonyms*–harmony, proportion, middle ground, steady, stabilize, level off

OR

Balance– *Antonyms*–imbalance, disproportion, instability, flightiness, self doubt, uncertainty, irrational, shakiness.

Scene Thirty-Eight

Helen at the Well

The miracle moment we all wait for.

Brother James: *I think we've started all over--*

Miss Annie: *Don't get up! Don't smooth anything else out for me, don't interfere in any way! I treat her like a seeing child because I ask her to see, I expect her to see, don't undo what I do!*

Captain Keller: *Where are you taking her?*

Miss Annie: *To make her fill this pitcher again!*

Aunt Ev: *You let her speak to you like that, Arthur? A creature who works for you?*

Captain Keller: *No, I don't.*

Brother Jimmy: *Let her go.*

Captain Keller: *What?*

Brother Jimmy: *I said -- let her go! She's right. She's right, Kate's right, I'm right, and you're wrong. Has it never occurred to you that on one occasion you might be consummately wrong?*

Miss Annie: *All right. Pump. No, she's not here. Pump. Water. W-a-t-e-r. Water. It has a name-- W-a-t...*

Helen: *Wah... wah. Wah... wah.*

Miss Annie: *Yes. Yes. Yes! Oh, my dear— (Helen falls to her knees, pats it, Miss Annie spells into it.). Ground. Yes! Pump. Yes! Yes! (Miss Annie spells) Tree. Step. Mrs. Keller! Mrs. Keller! Bell. Mrs. Keller! Mrs. Keller... Mrs. Keller. Mother. Papa-- She knows!*

Miss Annie's Memory of 'The Moment'

"We went out to the pump-house, and I made Helen hold her mug under the spout while I pumped. As the cold water gushed forth filling the mug, I spelled w-a-t-e-r in Helen's free hand. The word coming so close upon the sensation of cold water rushing over her hand seemed to startle her.

She dropped the mug and stood as one transfixed. A new light came into her face. She spelled 'water' several times. Then she dropped on the ground and asked for its name and pointed to the pump and the trellis, and suddenly turning round she asked for my name. I spelled 'teacher'."

Annie Sullivan, Story of My life. p265.

"Helen has taken the second great step in her education. She has learned that everything has a name, and that the manual alphabet is the key to everything she wants to know."

Annie Sullivan. Story of My Life. p 264

Helen's Memory of 'The Moment'

"As the cool stream gushed over one hand she spelled into the other the word water, first slowly then rapidly. I stood still, my whole attention fixed upon the motions of her fingers. Suddenly I felt a misty consciousness as of something forgotten—a thrill of returning thought; and somehow the mystery of language was revealed to me. I knew then that 'w-a-t-e-r' meant the wonderful cool something that was flowing over my hand. That living word awakened my soul, gave it light, hope, joy, set it free! There were barriers still, it is true, but barriers that could in time be swept away."

Helen Keller, The Story of My Life. p.17

"Thus I came up out of Egypt and stood before Sinai, and a power divine touched my spirit and gave it sight, so that I beheld many wonders. And from the sacred mountain I heard a voice which said, 'Knowledge is love and light and vision."

Helen Keller, Story of My Life. p.14.

What a Miracle Worker Would Share

I think at this very moment we all heard the Angels. *"Ahhhh!"*

We all have them - those *"Aha"* moments. Actually all day, everyday we experience *"Aha"* moments. Do you believe this? Listen and watch the different interactions in any given day. Ask questions and discover something you didn't know. The *'Aha'* moment may be heard as an *"Oh!?"* Even Miss Annie said *"Oh, my dear"* when she realized Helen actually connected words to meaning for the first time. Miss Annie felt the shift in that exact moment with Helen.

Notice every question you ask, especially those when you say – *'I don't understand...'* You may certainly not understand why the road turned that way or why the line was over here and not there. Or why the 'special' didn't include... Or why they said no, or why they said yes. Or why this and why that. Admit we don't have all the answers and admit that when we did get the answer we may have felt just a little bit stupid when we finally understood. Truthfully, matched energy? We may have asked the question a little condescending ourselves trying to make someone else feel stupid as if they didn't know what 'they' were doing!

We don't have to have all the answers all the time. Persevere, enjoy the journey, do what you can, know when to step up and know when to step back. Know when you are empowering and know how not to enable. Know when to play and have fun in this unusual opportunity/ challenge called life. Know when to go to the well!

> *"So I want to say to those who are trying to learn to speak and those who are teaching them: Be of good cheer. Do not think of to-day's failures, but of the success that may come to-morrow. You have set yourselves a difficult task, but you will succeed if you persevere; and you will find a joy in overcoming obstacles- a delight in climbing rugged paths, which you would perhaps never know if you did not sometime slip backward- if the road was always smooth and pleasant. Remember, no effort that we make to attain something beautiful is ever lost. Sometimes, somewhere, somehow we shall find that which we seek. We shall speak, yes, and sing too, as God intended we should speak and sing."*
> **Helen Keller The Story of My Life, p. 353**

Resounding -- *"Ahhhhhhh"* from all of us Angels!

About the Author

Anna P. Sweetnam Ph.D. owner and creator of The Conscious Connection in Ozona, FL. has been in the education field since 1979. With a Masters Degree in Special Education and a Ph.D. in Metaphysics she is uniquely qualified to address Spiritual growth and conscious awareness for the 21st Century. Dr. Anna shares deep insight and guidance using her Spiritual and intuitive consulting background encouraging individuals to be pure essence.